*A Spirituality of Survival*

# A Spirituality of Survival

## Enabling a response to trauma and abuse

*Barbara Glasson*

continuum

**Published by the Continuum International Publishing Group**

The Tower Building, 11 York Road, London SE1 7NX

80 Maiden Lane, Suite 704, New York NY 10038

www.continuumbooks.com

Scripture quotations taken from the New Revised Standard Version of the Bible, copyright © 1989 by the Division of Christian Education of the National Council of the Churches of Christ in the USA. Used by permission. All rights reserved.

Scripture quotations taken from the HOLY BIBLE, NEW INTERNATIONAL VERSION are copyright © 1973, 1978, 1984 by International Bible Society. Used by permission of Hodder & Stoughton Publishers, a member of the Hachette Livre UK Group. All rights reserved. 'NIV' is a registered trademark of International Bible Society.

First published 2009

British Library Cataloguing-in-Publication Data
A catalogue record for this book is available from the British Library.

ISBN: 978–1–4411–9255–4

Designed and typeset by Kenneth Burnley, Wirral, Cheshire
Printed and bound in Great Britain by Ashford Colour Press Ltd, Gosport, Hampshire

# Contents

# Preface

Living with our questions is a sign of being secure enough in God's company to wrestle with the things that are confusing or troubling. I believe we are greatly indebted to the disciple Thomas for permission to doubt. I understand doubt to be a hallmark of faith, rather than the opposite. This book is my story of living with a very big question, 'What does it mean to survive?' It is indeed a wrestling, not a conclusive theory. I hope simply to open windows, to provide glimpses of a spirituality born out of the struggle – both mine and others who have lived with the question for much longer than I have.

There are two parts to my job. I am both a Methodist minister in Liverpool city centre, and also the Director of the *face2face* project based at Holy Rood House, Centre for Theology and Health, in Thirsk, North Yorkshire. In Liverpool, I work alongside an emerging church community called 'Somewhere Else' which makes bread together, and at Holy Rood I am producing educational material for churches around the issues associated with sexual abuse. In Liverpool I am in the heart of a big city and in Thirsk I look out at the rolling hills. While these experiences of Church are radically and wonderfully different, they have both presented questions born out of encounters with people who survive.

Over the past two years I have been travelling with this question, as if it has been tucked in with my luggage. The journey has accompanied me around the streets of Liverpool in its transformation to

'European Capital of Culture 2008'. I have pondered it as I have sat with my elderly mother who represents a generation of strong women who survived the Second World War. I have taken this question with me to South Africa as I visited emerging bread-making communities in Soweto and also listened to some amazing people finding integration and healing through the story-telling process in the townships. And I have been privileged to accompany a group of 'survivors' to listen to similar stories in South America. In the middle of it all, I have taken time with Laura on her Derbyshire allotment, as we have listened to the growing patterns of the earth among her potatoes and beetroot.

I have had the hunch that individuals who have survived things hold a key to what it might mean to survive as nations and communities. I have begun my questioning by going to the root of the word 'survive'. It is a tricky word. Survival can denote a fingertip emergence to catch breath among the forces that threaten to overwhelm us, or a triumphant bursting forth into new life. The word 'survivor' can imply a helpless victim or a feisty freedom fighter. So I have wondered what does it mean to '*sur vivre*' – that is, 'live above' our experiences of trauma or abuse rather than '*sous vivre*', to be overwhelmed by them. And in this journey to discover the stories that '*sur vivre*' I have begun to discern a process of hope in which safe enough space can be discovered, bonds broken and individuals and communities find the resilience to live.

Within this journey I have also re-connected with the narrative of Luke and Acts. In particular, I have re-read the account from the perspective of 'being lost' and discovered new insights as we begin to read the story from underneath. This has been a tough wrestling with the scriptures, always trying to keep 'survivor's eyes' and struggling for an honest dialogue with the text. In particular, I have worked with the motifs of victim, silence and innocent suffering in the life of Jesus. Maybe my question about survival raises more questions than answers!

I have seen how the Gospel of Luke flows over into the Acts of the Apostles, and I have asked questions about surviving Church – a deliciously ambiguous phrase – as we realize that church communities often overlook the needs of the vulnerable. I see that a real engagement with those who have suffered trauma and abuse is the key to our understanding of mission, especially when we reflect that the silence of God signifies the attentiveness of God rather than God's absence. The writing of this book has sometimes felt like trying to find the 'Theory of Everything' as I have taken my question to individuals, town planners, environmentalists and policy-makers. Maybe it can do little more than provoke a conversation – I certainly hope it will!

For free material and further information on survivor issues, go to www.holyroodhouse.org.uk and follow the *face2face* link.

# Acknowledgements

Thank you to everyone who has helped with the writing of this book:

Sheila and Chris who made the trip to South Africa.
Revd Ike Moabi and his wife Ruth who were our hosts.
Bishop Paul Verryn of Joahnnesburg Central Mission.
The Volmoed Community for generous hospitality and conversation.

Steve, Heather, Marie, Vikki and Jo who made the trip to South America.
Thanks to Col, who made a different journey by staying at home!
Alison, Chris, Luke and Bethan who hosted us in Chile.
Bishop Nellie Ritchie and Rachel Starr who hosted us in Argentina.
Revd Tom Quenet and Revd Gary Hall and Formation in World Mission Committee of the Methodist Church, UK.

Laura, for times on her allotment and conversations about 'becoming'.

Donald and Kerstin for encouragement hospitality.

David, Emma, Robin and Alistair and Granny Jo for being my family.

All the odd bods at 'Somewhere Else'!

The therapeutic and staff team at Holy Rood House, Thirsk, especially Penny for collaboration on survivor retreats, also Anne, Fiona and Michelle.

Revds Elizabeth and Stanley Baxter for having the vision for this important work, and for their wisdom and encouragement.

The Epworth Fund for sponsorship and support.

*Barbara Glasson*

*For anyone who got up this morning,*
*noticed they were still alive,*
*and wondered what it meant.*

# Chapter 1

## The Hearing

Let us consider what it means to survive.

We are sitting on a simple bench in a barn-like building. The floor is mud. Around the walls and across the centre of the room are more benches. At the front is a plain wooden table with a jug of water and some plastic cups. We have been greeted with some traditional African handshakes, everyone is singing. We have been invited to bear witness to a hearing of Khulumani, part of the truth and reconciliation process in South Africa – 'Khulumani' means 'speaking out'.

As the singing quietens, one middle-aged woman makes her way to the bench, her head wrapped in a tight African head-dress. She speaks of how, during the days of apartheid, she had been kicked by the security forces as she knelt outside the prison where her son was detained, of the operations she had endured to try to remedy the brain damage the boots had caused, and of how she is bringing up grandchildren after her pregnant daughter was killed by a kick to the stomach. She tells her story simply and, through an interpreter, we hear her pain. When she has finished, a silence hangs in the room and then the community around her begin to sing a song she has chosen. The words of the song are 'God of opportunities, use me'.

Over the course of the next two hours we hear more stories as women and men make their way to the 'listening bench'. A mother tells of how her two children, shot by other children, died in the truck on the way to the hospital. A young man shows the scars he

1

sustained when a truck reversed over him on the night Nelson Mandela was released. A young woman tells of a corrupt building company that had shot her husband at the gate of their house during the recent reconstruction process in the townships.

As the stories are told, a leader of the Khulumani organization moves forward to be beside the tellers and gently massages their neck or gives a glass of water if the story becomes too painful. 'It's like giving birth', the counsellor says afterwards; 'there is a right time for these stories to be told and it is a labour.' Certainly we could see how he, and the women and men of that rural community, acted as midwives to each other. It felt like a very basic delivery room.

I am on a journey to discover what helps people '*sur vivre*'; that is, what helps stories to surface and enables people to claim their lives after they have experienced trauma or abuse. I am using the French root of the word 'survive' to distinguish this process of '*sur vivre*' (*vivre* = to live, *sur* = above or on top) as opposed to '*sous vivre*' (*sous* = below or underneath). The word 'survivor' can give so many mixed messages. If we think of surviving, it can denote either a life lived while others died, or a life claimed despite the destructive powers of death. In distinguishing '*sur vivre*' from '*sous vivre*' I want to affirm the life-giving possibility of a story surfacing from under the circumstances that have suppressed it. '*Sur vivre*' is not about pure survival, a desperate attempt to keep one's head above water, but rather speaks of a process of flourishing. Survivors are so much more than just survivors, they have important stories to tell which need attending to, not just for themselves but for the healing of communities and nations. '*Sur vivre*' is about seeing the world differently and finding possibilities for all of us to live in a new way.

Over the last two years I have travelled to various parts of the world and within my own localities with this question, 'What does it mean to survive?' Within these journeys I have looked for connections between the process of '*sur vivre*' for individuals, nations, neighbourhoods and the earth. While I have travelled, I have listened to many stories and sat alongside various groups, conversed with some of the midwives of the story-telling and tried to connect with my own issues.

I have also taken time to sit in the middle of the Derbyshire country-side with my friend Laura, an artist and allotment keeper who attends to the lessons that the natural environment communicates. On this journey I became increasingly aware how difficult it is for the subject of survival, '*sur vivre*', to be discussed. Often people prefer to remain silent than to disclose what has happened to them or to those around them. But when stories do surface, and if they are attended to with compassion and insight, then I have also seen massive potential for a new way of engagement, one that speaks to me of life and faith. Understanding something of what enables people to survive has shown me a new hope among the most fragile and vulnerable people of the earth, which is both a small and massive undertaking.

## '*Sous vivre*'

If '*sur vivre*' is to live 'above' a story of abuse, then '*sous vivre*' is to be the victim of a terrible silence.

Abuse is about the misuse of power. Wherever in the world abuses happen, there can be an awful silence. It is as if the trauma cannot be reduced to the logic that words require. So, the first thing I have tried to do on my travels is to listen out for the things that are not being said – for the absences, the silences, the deadly cycles of '*sous vivre*'.

One week in every month I work for a project called *face2face*. The *face2face* initiative has the intention of listening to the silence of survivors of sexual abuse within faith communities and is based at a centre for therapeutic healing and wholeness at Holy Rood House in Thirsk. Day by day a team of trained volunteer counsellors takes time with clients who are beginning to unravel their stories. It is a patient and skilled process. Many accounts are blurred, maybe abuse happened in early childhood and is only recalled in fragments and flashbacks. Sometimes the events are so painful that they can be expressed only in the third person. Often words give way to self-harm in order for the trauma to become manageable. In the privacy of counselling rooms, therapists hear of women and men raped by parents or siblings, of the rituals of abuse performed by cults or in the name of the Church, of babies aborted or given up to the terrors of abusive practices. Around all this lies the fear that has been instilled in those who are experiencing abuse should they ever disclose what happened: fear of people for whom they often still have a loyalty and sometimes still love. Because abuse is about power, and because abusers hold the power to silence their victims, abuse is also about silence and the silenced. Abuse suppresses stories. What happens in the therapeutic environment at Holy Rood House is an engagement with these silences, to the stories that have been forced to be covered up, to '*sous vivre*'.

This suppression of stories is a complex issue. In the case of individuals who have experienced abuse it may be that the grooming process has been so thorough that the fear of speaking is overwhelming. Grooming usually happens over a period of time. The individual is systematically isolated and networks of confidantes reduced or obliterated. There will probably be threats and bribes to ensure that the abused person remains quiet, and the silencing is compounded by an overwhelming sense of guilt. On the other hand, it may be that the person does not realize there is anything strange about the experience, particularly if it happened in early childhood. It is only later in life that most of us realize that our families might not be as 'normal' as we had assumed when we were growing up! One woman who spoke to me told me of her mother who was so emotionally damaged that she never held her children and expected them to care for themselves by the age of seven. This woman could only name the depth of that loss of maternal care as she raised her own children and learned how to hold and nurture them. Another woman had never met a man who had not abused her and led her life avoiding male friendship. Abuse silences because of the grooming process or because it becomes impossible for the person experiencing abuse to engage with any sense of what is normal.

This isolation, loss of normality and grooming leads to the separation of victims from any sense of autonomy or worth. It is for this reason that stories are often heard in isolation. In British society the bringing to birth of these stories is often in the therapeutic context.

The story-telling can be a privatized and confidential act, unlike the community processes we witnessed in South Africa. The growth in person-centred counselling in the UK has been remarkable over the last few decades and the need to find safe spaces in which to talk and be heard have caused a burgeoning of therapeutic services and time spent in doctors' surgeries. The 'birthing' of stories tends to be a private process as people who have experienced abuse seek safe enough spaces to share what has happened to them. '*Sur vivre*', then, can be an individual or a collective story-telling according to cultural mores or context. The attending to the silences around us requires an engagement with both individuals and communities, but also with our culture. Silences can also be held at national level; there are things that are simply not talked about or are assumed to be normal because they are part of a collective history.

In Britain we are a country of individuals with a collective story of survival, but we rarely talk about it. The 'winning' of the Second World War has resulted in a whole generation of British men and women, now in their eighties, who rarely speak of the trauma and loss. Among the elderly we see glimpses of a generation within which every family was bereft of relations, friends and property. Unlike Germany and indeed South Africa, Britain has not had to face a collective guilt and begin to speak of the horrors witnessed by us as a whole nation. On the whole we just 'Don't mention the war' and our remembering is often ritualized into wreath-laying and contrived silences. This collective silence has not, to my knowledge, been a source of therapeutic concern. How would it be possible to hear a whole generation of elderly people? We have been culturally attuned to accept this silence. If we are going to engage with what '*sous vivre*' is and begin to discern how it might be possible to '*sur vivre*', we will need special, culturally tuned antennae that enable us to hear what we are not hearing.

Further, it is not just individual people who are abused, or even distinct communities or nations – it is the earth, the environment, our surroundings. Waste-heaps around Johannesburg tell a story of profligate mining that has not been mindful of the survival and flourishing of the earth. Cyanide from mining explosives leaches into the water supplies, and other toxic substances are breathed in with the dust. This scarring and spoiling of the landscape brings its own implications for the future of the local people and for the future of the earth. These soil mountains stand in silent judgement over the powers of short-term advantage that are the legacy of colonialism and capitalism. The cost of abuse of the earth is a hot topic, within which we are also called to attend to what is not being said.

So, there are silences around at every level. The individual silences of the abused whose tongues are bound through fear and threat, the collective silencing of a whole society such as the people of Chile and Argentina where silence runs through national experience, and the silence of the earth as it stands spoiled and accusatory at the edges of our landscapes. Abuse is about power, and it silences all of us – individually, collectively and environmentally. We cannot engage with the process of '*sur vivre*' unless we understand those forces that lead to death, destruction and '*sous vivre*'. As I have travelled and listened and pondered on these things, I have begun to realize that this journey has significance not just for individuals but for our collective sustainability of the earth. If we are to '*sur vivre*' then we must begin to acknowledge this need to allow the stories to surface – fearlessly, remorsefully, searingly but also gently and lovingly, as the Khulumani counsellors have already discovered.

It was with all this in mind that I went this week to sit on Laura's allotment. Well, it's less of an allotment and more of a field. There are eight allotments altogether on the Chatsworth estate; seven are laid out in neat rows, with precision planted beans and regimented beetroot. Then there is Laura's. Laura has planted her seeds and is now in the business of listening to what they have to say to her. Laura is an artist and is considering the processes of 'becoming'.

At one end of Laura's allotment some tall artichokes are producing deep roots under the sandy soil. A tangle of raspberries crowds another corner, and a tree that has been laden with plums begins to lose its leaves as autumn begins to bite. She has harvested the peas but because their pods are a beautiful deep purple she has left them on the plant. There is a compost heap and a pile of sticks drying for kindling. The beetroot are a disaster, but she is leaving them in the soil anyway to see what happens. Between the vegetables, herbs grow wild and untended. We dig up some pink potatoes, their flesh creamy white, and we converse as we make a stew in her garden shed.

Chopping artichokes into the pan of boiling water, we talk about the allotment, not as a thing but as a process of becoming. It is not something to be 'managed' but to be 'attended to'. It is quite clear that Laura has a loving relationship with this allotment, it tells her things and she is listening to it. As I sit on the small wooden seat in the allotment shed, spooning a stew made of freshly dug vegetables and herbs, I am mindful of the similar wooden bench in South Africa where I have so recently listened to stories of abuse and violence. I begin to feel the power in these small, radical steps of attentiveness as Laura and I chat and listen to the Derbyshire rain soaking into the earth.

After the Khulumani listening process, we sat with the counsellor at a motorway service station, somewhat dazed by what we had heard and needing time to process our thoughts. He told us that he attends such hearings every week. 'How else will the nations be healed?' he asks. In Laura's shed I remember the words in Revelation that his words have echoed, 'The leaves of the trees are for the healing of the nations'. Within the Khulumani process, on Laura's allotment, at Holy Rood House and with my church community in Liverpool, I begin to understand that this healing, this listening, this attentiveness is a process of hard work, like giving birth. But it is essential work: the journey from 'sous vivre' to 'sur vivre' will take time, care and the willingness to listen to one another and to what is coming to birth among us.

As I have travelled with the question, 'What does it mean to survive?', I have not only recognized a way of possibility that I want to describe as 'sur vivre' but I also see that this question is a question about faith. St Paul writes of the whole earth 'groaning in travail' and I begin to make a connection between the birth-pangs of 'sur vivre' that I am encountering and the process of incarnation described in the Gospels. As a theologian and human being I see that this process is a faith imperative because I believe in a gospel that calls us to 'life in all its fullness'. This is not just divine wishful thinking but the call to live our lives on top of oppression and abuse and enable others to do the same. If abuse is about the deadly effect of misappropriated power, then I believe that God calls forth life, life from under the oppressions that seek to crush us, and begins to give voice to another way. God desires us to live in a way that subverts abuses. God's way is not a way of death, but a way to flourish. So I have turned to the Gospels, in particular the Gospel of Luke, to search for clues of God's message of '*sur vivre*'. This has been one of the most challenging parts of the journey! There have been times when I have felt overwhelmed by the motifs of victim and sacrifice. But I have discovered a sense in which the Gospel also survives as it begins to tell its story afresh above the weight of a lot of doctrinal assumptions and church baggage. I have been surprised by how often discovering what it means to '*sur vivre*' in relation to the story of God has brought me to a new sense of mission, a way of unbinding the story and enabling it to live in new ways, enabling a spirituality of survival.

## The bind

The deadly cycles of '*sous vivre*' suppress the human spirit, bring negativity, fear and foreboding. '*Sous vivre*' is about death – physical, emotional or spiritual – and, like most deaths, results in a binding, a shrouding of life. In these deadly cycles of abuse the powerful overcome, overwhelm or smother the less powerful, putting them into a position where their own power is bound, and they are trapped. Most often the first thing to be bound is the tongue. Individuals who have experienced abuse consistently recount the terrors of the threats they received 'not to tell'. In the Churches Together in Britain and Ireland publication, *Time for Action*, we read:

Commonly those who abuse children instil a fear that is so awful that a survivor knows almost instinctively that he or she cannot possibly dare tell another person about what has happened or is happening. Consequently there are deep-rooted feelings of loneliness, isolation and fear.[1]

Such feelings often last well into adulthood. It is not unusual for adults who have experienced abuse to continue to believe that they are totally in the power of the offender, even after the person who abused them has died. Many sexual abusers are skilled manipulators, and the use of secrecy and silencing has been well documented by specialists who treat such offenders. Techniques include telling children things that will frighten them, such as 'Your mother will have a heart attack if you tell' or 'You will go to prison if you tell' and other messages that will bind someone's tongue. All these messages are given to terrorize the person being abused into complete silence and to encourage compliance. Sex offenders within the clergy often use spiritual threats of confusing messages, such as: 'You'll go to hell if you tell', 'God does not mind what is happening', 'You will hurt God if you tell', or 'No one will believe you because I'm a priest.' Even when people are adult, independent and free to speak, the sense of being unable to disclose can still have the power to bind.

We need to be aware that most abuses happen in the home and by family members. Children abused by parents will already love those parents and be anxious to please. They will also respect the authority of a parent or sibling not to disclose, and the biggest threat is that love will be withdrawn. Within the cycles of sexual, emotional and physical abuses there is tied a convoluted knot of love and power which binds the tongues of those affected by trauma. The loci of silencing frequently violate the very places that should be safest to speak out without fear.

Similarly, in political oppressions, the power to silence and bind is often close to home. In South Africa the networks of trust were systematically broken down by the apartheid regime so that neighbours became informers on neighbours, church members on pastors, and children on teachers. Abused people soon learn to hold their tongues. During the Khulumani hearing we repeatedly heard stories of fear in connection with the police and security forces, but also in relation to friends, family and neighbours. Abuses of power infiltrated every level of social engagement so that it became impossible to know whom to trust. One person told of the advice given to them by an elderly priest, 'Say to no one what you cannot say to everyone.' In this environment of suspicion and mistrust, a society of fear was soon engendered and permeated every level of life.

This knot of silencing also binds communities and individuals in relation to the environment. The relocated 'Cape Coloureds', displaced from the townships, have been rehoused on the Cape Flats which are the areas most likely to flood in heavy rains. The exploited black workers of the Johannesburg mines were powerless to complain about the spoil-heaps that overshadowed their already impoverished neighbourhood because their livelihood depended on the mines. Those whose relatives had 'disappeared' in South America did not know whom to trust in their search. Who can stand up to individuals or political regimes that hold such power by force and bind the tongue of protest?

Among the victims of the world there are terrible silences, tongues are tied and words are trapped in cycles of oppression. Individuals, communities and nations can be caught up by these complex ties, resulting in both individual isolation and social exclusion. To understand '*sous vivre*' we have to begin to attend to these silences. It is only if we can begin to discover what is bound that we are able to speak of 'unbinding'.

## Unbinding

Abuse is about the misuse of power and it leads to silence and the binding of individuals to perpetrators in cycles of violence. This binding is of the whole body, but particularly the tongue which is rendered speechless either through fear of reprisal or mental disintegration. This power of others to silence can become all pervading. Fears and terrors can haunt and dement. In the UK, one in three girls is sexually abused before the age of 18, one in six boys before the age of 16.[2] There is a mighty silence in every gathering of humankind. People who are experiencing abuse are not marked out as special beings, behaving strangely or unable to cope with life, they are everywhere holding onto deep silences in the context of seemingly ordinary lives. Individuals have been groomed to bear this silence in isolation, they have often had support networks undermined and are unable to trust disclosure. Political abuses work in similar ways by undermining the infrastructure of trust. Police forces and the military may be in the pay of the abusers, and informers can come clothed as friends. This great silence suppresses the fullness of life which is God's intention both to individuals and to the earth. There is a sense of powerlessness, of nothingness. The poorest communities of the world sense they are out of sight, invisible, of no consequence. Silence and nothingness go hand in hand, and there is a disintegration of any feeling of autonomy or worth. Indeed, many people who '*sous vivre*' lose sight of being individuals but live in a fragmented psyche in which dissociation makes integration of experiences seemingly impossible. Similarly, with the undermining of trust in political oppressions, there is disintegration and worthlessness. So, where is God in all this? It might be easy to say, 'This is nothing to do with God', maybe God is also nothing? Are we to preach a counsel of despair to those victimized and alone? Certainly the Church has often done much to compound the sense of guilt in those who are suppressed and repressed by violence and abuse. How is it possible for victims to live on top of this oppression, to '*sur vivre*', and what is God's place in the process?

Ten years ago when my friend Alison swallowed a bottle of paracetamol and jumped from a bridge into moving traffic, she lay in a hospital bed looking more dead than any living person I have seen. Her spine was crushed but the depression that had caused her suicide attempt had lifted. Later, when I asked her where she thought God had been when she jumped, she replied in a matter-of-fact way, 'Oh, beside me on the bridge.' Some God, I thought, that didn't intervene, didn't speak out, didn't pull her back from the brink. I was extremely angry with God for not rescuing her and preventing her excruciating pain and despair. But not Alison, for her God was present and remains present, even in the face of nothingness. This is not necessarily the case for all victims. Often God is most notable for God's absence. How hard it is to believe in a silent God, within the awful silence of violence and abuse. Is this not the callous God of infinite superiority and detachment?

Does God's silence mean God's absence? Has Jesus, in fact, been abandoned by God at the point of crucifixion? It may appear so, yet belief in a God of infinite mercy and transforming love means I still hold on to the belief that there is no place from which God is absent. God is infinitely present to all creation, pervading the cracks and darkness as well as the highs and hopes. So how is God present in the silence and binding of abuse, and in what way do we come to understand this presence to signify a God of mercy and love?

One day when Alison, my suicidal friend, was in hospital fighting for her life, I found myself in the hospital car park waiting for the beginning of visiting time. I was angry, anxious, mixed-up and fearful of what I was going to say when I went onto the ward. It was then that I noticed the letters on the number plates of the two cars opposite me – one said 'HUG' and the other said 'GAG'. While I don't believe in a God who strategically places number plates, I do think there was wisdom in my seeing that these were two messages pertinent to my impending visit, first to embrace the situation and second to wait in the silence without ditching my own stuff. As a friend advised me later, 'Don't just *do* something Barbara, stand there!' Just as my silence indicated my total engagement with the relationship and suffering I held with my friend, I believe that God's silence signifies not absence, but total engagement. God becomes silent in order to be with the silenced. It is an ultimate act of love to be able to enter the awful silence and suffer together.

How does being silent with the silenced signify an infinite response of love? Silence can be a very deep place. There is the silence that results from the binding of the tongue and there is the silence of deep attention, when all we can do is 'be there'. The meeting of these silences, the meeting of the silenced and those who attend to the silence, is the place where '*sous vivre*' encounters '*sur vivre*'. I am beginning to understand that it is only when we enter into the silence at the heart of ourselves that we are able to give proper attention to the silence at the heart of creation. This silence is different from the terrible silence of the abused. It is a silence of longing and empathy in which words have failed and an embodied, rather than a spoken, response is necessary – it is the silence of '*sur vivre*' rather than the silence of '*sous vivre*'. Being in this silence, and attending to the pain of alienation and silencing that all people who suffer abuses know, is a sign of the power of transformation. In this place where the silences meet, there is a safe enough place for the ties around the tongue of the abused person to be loosened.

It is in this place that we realize that we are not 'sufferer' and 'friend' but rather two people who are being attended to by the same God. Just as we can be silent because we are listening, so also God is silent because God is listening, listening with the very being of God's self, in the abyss of silence, redeeming the silence, bringing the words to birth. It is at this place, where the silences meet, that the process of '*sur vivre*', of bringing a story to birth, is initiated. Jesus is the pivot between '*sous vivre*' and '*sur vivre*', between a deadly silence and the birth of a life-giving story, between death and life. God can unbind tongues with Pentecostal force, not through powerful speech but through divine listening. The silence of God is the life-giving longing of God. Alison knew this when she jumped from the bridge – God was there, not as divine manipulator or rescuer, but as aching, silent, incarnate friend.

This labour of '*sur vivre*' is started not by the story-telling, but within the meeting of the silences, the meeting of the silenced with the infinite silence of God. This meeting is the initiation of a process that results in the birth of a story, and it is the emergence of this story that brings life from underneath abuse and oppression. But story alone is not the beginning of survival; the meeting of the silences is the beginning. And at the heart of this process is the God of silence. This silent God is not an absent God but a listening God. God's presence is within the depth of the silence, such a silence is the ultimate solidarity of love. It is the hope that God will relinquish the power of speech in order to unbind the silences of the earth and the people of the earth and bring them to birth.

But do we really want to believe in the transformative power of a silent God?

On my journey I have discovered that people of faith do a lot of talking about God, praying to God and, on a good day, listening to God – but they rarely sense the presence of the silent, listening God. Little space is given to God as the great silence surrounding the earth, the longing for the story of humankind to be born, the infinite waiting that is paying attention to the travail of creation and created beings. We are mostly far too busy to have any sense of the God who is listening to us. And isn't the Bible rather about God speaking to his people and our struggles to discern what he is saying and our disobedience to a whole set of clear instructions? How are we to live our lives in the presence of a silent God who meets us before the story-telling, before the word, and who hangs around with us in a place where silence meets the silenced?

As we begin reading the scriptures with an eye to the process of 'sur vivre', we need to look again at the places where Jesus is silent and is silenced. In this way we might begin reading the story 'from underneath' and observe how he has lived a life both as a silenced victim and as a survivor. This 'reading from underneath' peels back the dominant narrative and reveals Jesus showing a way to bring the silenced voices of the world to light. Jesus is found entering a place of the deepest, eternal silence and then unbinding the tongues of those who were betrayed, abandoned and lost.

## Being born from silence

At the beginning of St Matthew's Gospel we learn that, very soon after his birth, there was a move to silence the baby Jesus. This move has euphemistically been referred to as 'The Slaughter of the Innocents'. The scale of this slaughter is not known but clearly what we hear described is an act of ethnic cleansing. In this story, and through the power of God and dreams, Jesus is not a victim of this act of silencing, but his contemporaries are, and we hear of the memory of 'Rachel weeping for her children and refusing to be consoled because they are no more' (Matthew 2.18). The silencing of a whole generation is a mass act of abuse, political and individual. The terror of the silent babies and the wailing of the lamenting mothers is the precursor to the proclamation of John the Baptist, a voice crying in the wilderness, 'Prepare the way of the Lord'. A voice crying in the context of the silence, the silence of the lost and the bereft, the silence of the wilderness.

Later we meet the adult Jesus himself coming out of this silent wilderness to proclaim the word of God, to speak, to preach, to minister, to pronounce. But later in Matthew's Gospel we learn of the death of John the Baptist, beheaded at the behest of Salome. John is the victim of ultimate silencing, of imprisonment, isolation and death. The words that Jesus proclaims are spoken into the context of silencing, of personal and political oppressions, of innocent suffering (Mark 6.16–29). Immediately after the death of John, Jesus retires to a deserted place.

Throughout the accounts of the life and ministry of Jesus we hear of this to-and-fro of engagement and subsequent withdrawal to the hills or to the sea, to be silent. The rhythm of speaking and listening brings a dynamic of relationship in which we sense the solitary nature of Jesus alongside the deeply personal and intimate encounters he initiates along the way. He has conversations with people made outcast by political exclusion, the Samaritans, victims of societal taboos, the mad and the leprous, those considered unclean such as the woman with the flow of blood (Luke 8.43–48) and those literally voiceless through dumbness. Jesus brings the stories of the silenced to light but he also withdraws into his own silence. In his life, in this to-and-fro, he embodies the divine person in whom the silences meet.

This is never more apparent than in the silence of Jesus before Pilate. Is he a victim at this point? Clearly he is at the mercy of the political and religious authorities whose intent is to silence him for good, but unlike many victims, he still has a choice to live. He could deny his allegiance to the gospel he has proclaimed and withdraw into the fabric of Palestine. He chooses, however, to remain silent before the power of the authorities. He knows that this silence will lead him to the ultimate silence of his death. Although he has not been silenced as many victims are, he chooses silence over speech. It is an embodied act of both the victim and the defiant. Later, in the garden of Gethsemane and on the cross, he will begin to wonder why the God of everything is also silent. Maybe there is no deeper silence in the history of the world than that of Easter Saturday; the tomb is sealed, there are no more choices, and there are no more words. People who have experienced abuse throughout the world will know of this silencing, a place where God is so silent that they sense they are in a place of ultimate desolation.

And yet also, in the place where the silenced and the silence meet, there is embodied, through Jesus, an eternal solidarity. He descended into hell, into our hell, into the place of nothingness, into the endless silence. The Word died and was silent so that the silent can give birth to words. Where the silences meet there begins the labour of new life. In the dark heart of the tomb a different story is being born. In this very darkness the transition from '*sous vivre*' to '*sur vivre*' is happening, a new way is coming to birth and, like all labours, it is a painful process.

## Annunciation

In the little wooden shed on the outskirts of Johannesburg, a man tells of his frustration with the processes of the new South African government. 'We longed for freedom, but now it has come it is not freedom'; and a woman laments her son, so traumatized by the experiences of apartheid that he is unable to settle anywhere and spends his life wandering the city streets. In a counselling room at Holy Rood House, a woman self-harms as the pain of a childhood memory cuts through her ability to find words. Alison learns how to use a wheelchair and live with the pain that is going to continue to pierce her body like hot needles for the rest of her life. Outside the tomb of Jesus a woman asks, 'Where have they taken my Lord?' and the answer to the question soon disappears into nothingness. So what is this transformation process that unbinds the tongue and begins to set free the stories of trauma and the songs of lament?

Someone said of the Khulumani counsellor, 'He is the message.' The transformation process is an embodied process in which people are prepared to enter into the place where the silenced meet the silence of God. These people are indeed the incarnate message, as embodied in Jesus, whether they know it or not. Being in silence with the silenced is a hard place indeed; how much easier for us to fill up our days with words, because words are a means of power, and silence takes us to a place of apparent powerlessness. Yet this process is, I believe, an imperative of the listening God. It is a mission imperative; by this I am not referring to a place of verbalizing doctrine or enlisting Christians, but rather a place where the God of silence is prepared to meet us within a dynamic of grace – an imperative of Missio Dei, of the God who goes ahead of us, even into the silence; it is the mission of the eternally silent, attentive, love-bearing, listening God.

It is the mission of the people of God to pay attention to this God who goes ahead, a mission to be present for the silenced and to embody the listening love of the Creator. As any trained listener will know, the process of 'hearing' involves a certain amount of 'self-emptying'. The clutter and chatter of our everyday lives needs to be quelled in order to have the space to give real attention to the stories that are being born among us. This kenosis is at the heart of the silencing of Jesus who chooses to be nothing in order to stand alongside the silenced of the earth, the silences of the earth. The self-emptying of Christ, through his crucifixion, is the re-entry of the powerful God into the time before the word, into silence, into chaos, into darkness, so that a re-creation can be resurrected. This is why listening is not simply the work of the therapist, but also the work of the missionary. If we believe in a God who listens, and in a Christ who has stepped into silence, as an eternal act of solidarity with the silenced of the earth, then what does this imply for discipleship and mission?

I want to suggest that it is the mission of those who seek to follow Jesus to have the bearing of such divine attentiveness. That, contrary to the perceived wisdom of evangelism as proclamation, we are called to become a community of believers who listen, who are attentive to the silences that are around us, the silences of people, the silences of creation. Our primary mission is to listen to the God who has chosen, through Jesus, to risk being nothing for the sake of our '*sur vivre*', as individuals and as a planet. Through Christ we are called to hear, to bear witness to those who groan in travail, to the silenced among us, to all that is missing and lost. This is not simply a piece of therapy, but an act of redemption. It is the work of God in the world.

Simone Weil writes,

> Not only does the love of God have attention for its substance, the love of neighbour, which we know to be the same love, is made of the same substance. Those who are unhappy have no need for anything in this world but people giving them attention. The capacity to give one's attention to a sufferer is a rare and difficult thing: it is almost a miracle, it is a miracle.[3]

Here is the connection between the God who enters into the deepest of silences and the call to mission. God's self-emptying brings an eternal attentiveness to creatures and to creation. God, through Jesus, relinquishes speech in order to be attentive to the silences of the world. God enters silence in order to call forth the words of the new creation, *in order for God's beloved creation to 'sur vivre'*. This holy attention is a call for us to pay attention to each other and to the earth as a redemptive action.

Nelle Morton asks, 'How many women and men have been rendered silent because the words just did not exist to "hear them into speech"? What is needed is a "hearing" engaged in by the whole body that evokes speech – a new speech – a new creation.'[4] This 'whole body' attentiveness has been borne out for us by the 'whole body' response of Jesus as he has willingly entered the silence of death and the tomb. And so the Church, as the body of Christ, is similarly called into engagement with divine attentiveness, to individuals and to Creation. The body is called, individually and collectively, to stand in solidarity with the silenced, to wait in the silence, to pay attention to the silence, to hold fast in the silence, to be the message, to remain silent – until the words can be brought to birth from the silenced.

As we sat with the counsellor on the simple wooden benches of a South African village, our backs ached from leaning forward to hear the words of the story-tellers, translated for us. We knew that we were witnesses to a powerfully redemptive act. By the commitment of Khulumani to sit and wait within the silence that is the pain of South Africa, a new way of being is being brought to light. A body language of redemption, among the women and men who collectively wait for stories to be born, it was physically and emotionally uncomfortable to hear the accounts of violations that were being told. It required the attention of our whole body. In the counselling rooms at Holy Rood House a similar process comes to birth as trained practitioners wait and prompt until the words begin to be spoken out of the depths of unspeakable silencing. It takes all the counsellor's wisdom and energy to pay such undivided attention. It is a 'whole body' listening that is required.

In the same way, the listening God has become an embodied expression of listening, through the silence of Jesus. This incarnational engagement bore the body scars of the God who waited within the silence of victimization and crucifixion. This is a costly process. And, as the body of Christ, the Church is called into such a role. It must learn to bear the marks of silent attentiveness to the victims of the earth, and to the earth.

As, in her allotment, Laura watches the plants flourish or fail, we are each called into the intense, exquisite, vivid attentiveness that calls forth life 'from underneath'. Some stories are born gently and under the cover of darkness, others are surgically assisted by prompting practitioners, some are delivered violently with convulsions of emotion, others stillborn and despairing. This is the work of God.

## 'Do not be afraid'

And so to Luke's Gospel; at the very beginning we hear of a series of announcements. The first is literally the binding and unbinding of a tongue as Zechariah is struck dumb at the news of the child to be born to him. After the conception of the baby, his wife Elizabeth was in seclusion; being childless had resulted in her being in a place of isolation and shame. It is not until she is visited by her pregnant cousin Mary that she exclaims, with a loud cry, 'Blessed are you among women, and blessed is the fruit of your womb. And why has this happened to me . . . ? For as soon as I heard the sound of your greeting, the child in my womb leapt for joy' (Luke 1.42–44). Hearing this exclamation, Mary begins her song of praise, Mary who has been disgraced and perplexed by her unlikely pregnancy. When Zechariah is eventually able to speak, he too begins to proclaim, seeing what is happening to him and his family as being part of the greater story of Israel. And he names the child, 'He will be called John'. This releasing of words continues, to the isolated shepherds on their hillside and to Simeon and Anna in the Temple.

In the wooden shed outside Johannesburg, as the women and men take their turns on the 'listening bench', the counsellor nods his head. One woman has told of how the security forces gave her father a slow poison while in prison, how her mother died of stress and how she was evicted from every house in which she tried to settle. She tells of how she was forced to sleep in the graveyard beside her father's grave, how even now she fights for the land rights to her family property. Her story of exclusion and suffering has been named, the silence has been broken.

At the end of the 'telling' the counsellor responds, 'You have suffered greatly, my mother. You have been treated like dog. Wicked men have killed your father and taken your land . . .' In the silence that follows, each of these 'tellers' knows that they have been heard. 'They have a need to annunciate . . .' says the counsellor. It seems a curious word to use. I wonder if he means 'enunciate', to spell out what has happened to them. But as I remember the story of the birth of Jesus, I return to 'the annunciation', the proclamation, the telling out. Yes, Khulumani means 'speaking out' but also signifies the message of angels, 'Do not be afraid.'

In a counselling room at Holy Rood House, a woman is talking in a strange voice. It is the voice of Jason – the name she has given to the personification of abuse. Through her dissociation and confusion she is beginning to discover the story of what has happened to her. The counsellor sits attentively within the process. These disclosures are hard to hear – and much harder to tell. This naming and telling comes with the delivery of the words, as the waters of silence are broken, as the hidden secrets come bawling or gasping into the daylight. Telling a story is a huge act of courage. Unless we are paying attention it may well be missed.

People who have experienced abuse will often wait years before they feel safe enough to begin to disclose. The exact timing of a story's arrival cannot be predicted. It may come out at an unexpected moment, bursting into a room with anger and chaotic behaviour. Whenever or however it happens, the need for the selected listener to pay proper attention and to set proper boundaries is crucial. But this does not mean that we all need to be trained counsellors; we just need to be aware of what we are doing and what we are not doing. Mostly, when we hear such a story we are simply being asked to believe it – even if it has inconsistencies. The issue at stake is not, 'Is this true?' but 'Are you listening?'

So, the process of '*sur vivre*' is one that begins with God, the God who is listening in silent attention to the earth and its people. Through Jesus, this loving attention is embodied. Jesus enters into the depths of divine silence in order to be with the silenced. This 'meeting of the silences' is the creative place in which stories are held and nurtured until such time as the labour of telling begins. This holding of silence is both the ministry of Jesus and the mission of the body of Christ in the Church and among the people of the earth. The movement from '*sous vivre*' to '*sur vivre*' begins with entry into this silence and a commitment to hold fast within the waiting until the words take flesh. This fleshing-out of stories is an annunciation, an announcement of a new life, a life without fear that can live from underneath oppression.

As for Mary, Elizabeth and Zechariah, this annunciation can come only after they are encouraged not to be afraid. Not being afraid is not a simple act of will; it is often a process of shaking off the messages of fear that have been learned and, in the case of abuse, taught from a very early age. The unbinding of tongues takes time, patience, skill and insight. But often the first telling of a story isn't in a counselling room on a listening bench but somehow 'in passing'. People who have experienced abuse may practise stories, test people out to see if they are to be trusted, talk in the third person, or give snippets of information to a friend. To be aware of God's attentiveness is not a remote theological theory but a mission prerogative. Churches and faith communities are called to be safe enough, boundaried places where the truth has space in which to be told and held. How we make such spaces of trust and acceptance is not simply a way of reordering the Church but also a way of reordering inner space to make room for the process of attentiveness; more a question of how we can 'be' Christians rather than people that 'do' stuff for God – and this is what I would like to consider in the next chapters. In particular I want to ponder prayer as silence, and liturgies as the work of the people. I want to investigate the processes that allow spaces to become safe and how we can be sensitive to thresholds and boundaries, how the bonds of oppressions can be broken and the liturgies of life sung.

But right now I am sitting on Laura's allotment, the first frosts are drawing patterns on the shrivelling leaves of the raspberry canes. The purple stalks of the beetroot begin to twist and become brittle; the blackbird tugs worms from under the artichokes. There is no knowing what seeds have already germinated or what will emerge next year. Now is the waiting time. We sit and consider Laura's theme of 'becoming' as we wrap our hands around mugs of warm coffee and blow steamy breath into the cold October afternoon.

## Chapter 2

# The Presenting

I am in the vestry of a church. I have been asked to take a funeral. It is not my church – the minister is away and I am covering for him. Elsie was a lady in her eighties, known to the church all her life and latterly through the Ladies' Circle. She was a spinster. I have visited her brother and sister and I have talked with the church steward to try to get the picture of what this woman was like. Despite my best efforts, I have gleaned very little information; the message from all of them was that 'Elsie struggled with her nerves.' I am also struggling with my nerves: two minutes before the service, I have little to go on to paint a picture of this life. I have one last desperate attempt at extracting information from the duty steward. 'I gather she suffered a lot from her nerves,' I lead hopefully. 'Yes,' she says, 'you know how it is in families, it was the father I think, all the children suffered in one way or another, you know how it is with fathers like that . . .' With that sudden insight, it is time to go into the church, the coffin has arrived . . .

'*Sur vivre*', surfacing above traumatic stories, begins when silence meets the silenced. As such, it is not an isolated activity, it requires company. But here is another bind. To seek safe company requires a huge amount of trust, and it is trust that has been most undermined in cycles of oppression and abuse. Those who should be trusted cannot be trusted. There is a need to locate a safe enough space before trust can be reinstated. This is more of a process than an event. We can assume that faith communities will provide a safe space for such conversations, but sadly these issues often remain hidden under a veneer of religious coping. So what makes a 'safe enough' space in which to tell a story, and how do we hear the clues that can bring stories to birth – preferably before the coffin is coming down the aisle of a church?

Before the transition from apartheid, many of the black and coloured communities of South Africa were 'relocated'. They were moved away to the edges of cities into poorly constructed flats and houses. Frustration and anger often erupted, and the beating and raping of women could be clearly heard through insubstantial walls. 'Of course,' said our companion, 'everyone hears, but nobody hears.' Fear of telling is real fear. Any number of angels saying 'Do not be afraid' are not going to sway the argument; fear is real, reprisals are likely and trust has to be earned by all communities, including faith communities. Whatever the context, naming what has happened, individually or collectively, is a dangerous activity. So when we talk of 'safe space' we need to take account of the real fears that come with telling. Safe spaces need to be located in both the physical and the emotional environment.

On the eighth day, Luke's Gospel tells us, the baby Jesus was named and presented in the Temple. In this place were two elderly people who had waited for this naming ceremony for a long time, Simeon and Anna. Simeon took the baby in his arms and sang out for joy because he could see that the story of Israel was being fulfilled. But his praise also has a coda. This child is destined to be rejected, translated as 'for the falling and rising of many' in the New International Version (Luke 2.34). The thoughts of hearts and souls will be laid bare and Mary's own heart will also be pierced. The old man is both joyful and chastening. He is wise enough to know that, when stories are told, when situations are named, trouble can happen and pain often ensues. Sometimes silence may seem to be the best option.

So, how do we hear what is not being said? How can we open safe enough spaces to give attention to the dynamics of joy and sorrow that such encounters bring? How can stories surface – '*sur vivre*' –

so that people and communities and environments can also survive?

I am going to deal with three questions concerning what makes a safer space. First, an exploration of the external factors that can provide a sense of being in a safe physical environment; second, a consideration of the inner factors that unlock the processes of '*sur vivre*'; and third, question how God embodies for us such safer spaces in the person of Jesus.

## External safe space

On arriving at Central Station in the centre of Liverpool – indeed, most of the way from leaving my suburban home on my journey to work – I am on security camera. A camera on the train watches to check if I am putting my feet on the seats, a camera watches to see if I am carrying any suspicious packages along the station platform, a camera watches my passage up Bold Street to my office, and a camera decides whether or not I will be allowed through the front door. Does this mean Liverpool is a safe or an unsafe place? In 2002 an alliance of the City Council, Merseytravel and Merseyside Police installed a total of 240 new digital cameras across the city centre and its main arterial routes with 70 miles of fibre-optic cable.

Between 1999 and 2003 Home Office spending on CCTV was anticipated to be in the order of £190 million. A *Guardian* article quotes Liverpool's Chief Inspector of the day, Mike Creer:

> It's about feelings of safety, public reassurance, public confidence. The whole reason for putting this in, at the end of the day, is to make people feel safer, to make people want to invest in the place, to make people want to come into the city, not only in their leisure time but for tourism as well.[1]

But the same article goes on to quote the National Crime Reduction Organisation (NACRO) report in which, of the 24 CCTV 'crime-busting' systems installed in 2002, only 13 were found to have coincided with a significant reduction in crime. In seven cases there was no detectable change, while in four instances crime had actually gone up. Most damningly perhaps, the Home Office's own surveys into the usefulness of the technology have suggested that something so simple as improving street lighting may be four times more effective in reducing crime.[2]

The UK has become the most watched, catalogued and categorized nation in the world. And the most popular reason given for this is to increase public safety. I think the jury is still out. My personal opinion is that surveillance means that Liverpool is neither safe nor unsafe – it simply means that on most of my way to work I am being watched.

In truth, there is no such thing as a completely safe space, nowhere in the world is completely safe. If, for example, a gang of thieves springs from a doorway as I make my way to work, they will almost certainly have snatched my bag and run off into the crowd before anyone spots them on CCTV and comes to help me. The quality of CCTV pictures is often too poor to see what is going on anyway. The purpose of the cameras is to make me *feel* safer as I walk through the city; and, I suppose, to make the opportunist thief a little more wary of being caught – if not actually in the act, then at a later date when films are produced as police evidence.

Certainly, for people who have experienced abuse, the language of 'surveillance' carries many mixed messages. Being watched can bring reassurance to some but terror to others – it all depends on who is watching. Feeling safe and being safe are two different things. Life is full of risks, and even if I were to stay at home all day with all the windows and doors locked, there is no guarantee I will not be struck by a mystery virus or a random earthquake. It is for this reason that I think it more useful to consider 'safe enough space'. If we leave the rhetoric of safety and consider what makes 'safe enough space' it gives the creative possibility of risk-taking, acknowledges the social dynamics of space, and gives a sense of collective responsibility at street level.

There are certain external factors that make a space feel 'safe enough', and as I have listened to the voices of people who have experienced trauma or abuse, I have heard some clues as to what these factors might be. These indicators might best be summarized as: a consideration of who holds the power, an awareness of exits and entrances, an acknowledgement of the place of memory, and an eye to scale. Even so, they will not be the same for everyone. What is safe enough for one person might be terrifying for another; but having said this, let us go on to consider how external spaces could possibly become 'safe enough'.

### Who holds the power?

If we remember that abuse is about the misuse of power, then safe enough spaces will be those that give a redistribution of power in favour of the vulnerable. This has to be a real and fair distribution, not an illusion constructed by the rhetoric of public order. Any understanding of 'safe enough space' needs to be linked to attitudes and policies of justice. Security cameras may give the impression of increased public safety, but what actually makes the street safer as I walk to work? I suggest that the answer to this question lies in an intricate web of social policy decisions that have little to do with security cameras.

For instance, if we consider that I have my bag snatched by a drug addict, the security camera will only deal with me, that individual thief and that particular bag. But an addict desperate for her next fix is part of a bigger picture, part of a whole web of social organization. So, in order to make city streets safe enough places, we need to ask whether there is a policy of treating drug addiction that helps addicts to be treated as humans rather than outlaws. This in turn leads to strategic government policy to consider whether addiction can be considered a medical issue rather than a criminal offence. Similarly, my safety is enhanced if I am not significantly and noticeably richer than or different from the people around me. Here we have a political issue concerning the fair and just distribution of wealth, housing policies and the attitude of the police to the street homeless. In the same way, my sense of safety is influenced by whether or not I am confident that the community around me is sufficiently public spirited to intervene if I get into difficulties. This brings into the safety debate the city's sense of community cohesion, identity and collective well-being. Ironically, in Liverpool this seems to be undermined by the security camera mentality, where the safety of strangers in the street becomes the responsibility of an invisible observer rather than visible passers-by. If I am to be safe enough, then others, including addicts, have to be safe enough too.

So, safer space is not about isolated individual instances, but about a redistribution of power in communities. The formation of external safer spaces is therefore a political and social agenda, rather than a push to privatize public space in which individuals may be made more vulnerable by the rhetoric of safety. Privatizing public space simply removes the powerful to the realm of invisibility and proffers an illusion of safety to the vulnerable that can actually make them more isolated and at risk. This poses dilemmas for town planners and architects who work with developing gated communities and shopping centres patrolled by security guards. It seems as if our external world of safety does not, ironically, enhance our ability to 'sur vivre', which is concerned with 'safe enough' physical spaces in which it becomes possible to take risks, rather than segregated spaces with the illusions of safety.

In the days of apartheid in South Africa, this rhetoric and surveillance became a sinister force. Whole areas, such as District 6 in Cape Town, were bulldozed overnight. Black and coloured communities were forcibly removed, and 'safety' meant segregation. In post-apartheid days the sale of electric gates and razor wire continued to soar. The concept of safety may no longer be policed by a repressive regime, but economic apartheid remains. South Africa has the largest gap between rich and poor of any developing country. In South Africa, as in the UK, the question of safety enters the political and social arena as well as person-to-person contact. The rebuilding of trust is a long, hard process, both in post-apartheid Cape Town and post-sectarian Liverpool. 'Sur vivre' will only become a reality when people take the risk of being 'safe enough'.

### *Where are the exits?*

If a sense of collective ownership, responsibility and community encourage spaces in which to feel safe enough at street level, how does it work in indoor spaces such as churches or offices? One important aspect of safe enough space is the ability to leave it. Whatever social situation we find ourselves in, we all need to know how to get out. A sense of safer space is enhanced if we are aware of entrances, exits and the thresholds in between. This is particularly relevant for people who have been trapped within cycles of abuse and shut in rooms, cupboards or cars while an assault has occurred. People who have been physically or emotionally bound by individuals or groups need to know that it is possible to escape and are justifiably wary of entering into spaces from which the exits are not clear. But spaces without escapes are physically and emotionally dangerous for everyone, not just for those who consider themselves survivors. It is a basic human need to have the power to enter and leave as we choose. It is for this reason that, if we want to create safe enough spaces, we need to ask questions about keys, doors and thresholds.

When I arrive at work, I am greeted by Dave the *Big Issue* vendor. We usually exchange a few words while I rummage in my bag for my keys. I let myself in and am soon on my way to my office. Being the key holder, I am empowered to get past the physical barrier of the front door; others must come and ring the bell. Dave usually keeps people talking while the person inside rushes for the entrance buzzer, but sometimes he lets other people in once the door is open. The power of exclusion and inclusion rests with the people on the inside and on the threshold. These thresholds are crucial because they represent places where the power is transferred. People who want to develop safe enough places have to be aware of this power and distribute it wisely. The symbol of this power is the key to the door.

Most organizations, not least churches, have arguments about who has the keys to the premises. Keys represent power, and those who have keys have access to power. Key holders are the ones who control the comings and goings. They are the ones who can exclude or ban. Key holders can keep people in and lock people out, and because they have this responsibility, they also have responsibility for a church being a safe enough space. And here is the crux of a lot of church council arguments: is the church to be a safe space (no broken light bulbs) or a safe enough space (we tolerate a degree of mess)? Churches that think they operate an open-door policy should count how many keys they have and then ask who carries them! I am not advocating spaces that are totally open – this is also an invitation to abuse – but I am suggesting that if we want safe enough space for people to flourish in an open environment of questioning faith, then the body language of our church buildings is crucial. I will talk more about barriers and thresholds in the next chapter. Safe enough spaces are those that interact with the people who use them – their needs, fears and memories.

### The naming of memories

Safe enough spaces need to name these memories and associations by acknowledging that they are linked in a variety of different ways with people's stories. Leonie Sandercock, a town planner in Vancouver, talks of the 'song lines' of the Aborigines in pre-colonial Australia, along a labyrinth of invisible pathways; these song lines link the human memory and story with the built environment. They trigger associations that give a sense of being rooted and help a place to feel 'safe enough':

> . . . the Aboriginals travelled (these song lines) in order to perform all those activities that are distinctly human – dance, marriage, exchange of ideas, and arrangements of territorial boundaries by agreement rather than by force. These song lines, in aboriginal culture, are what sustain life. The task of a new planning imagination is to search for the city's song lines, for all that is life sustaining, in the face of the inferno.[3]

There is a new shopping centre in the middle of Liverpool – the Met Quarter. It is notable because it is probably the only place in town where it is (theoretically!) possible to buy £200 shoes. The Met Quarter represents much of what redevelopment offers – the chance to buy named brands and associate with the carefully crafted ambience of a modern mall. It is well lit, and has a range of designer outlets and upmarket coffee shops. In the central well of the mall are long leather sofas and luxuriant palms. What the locals remember about the Met Quarter is that it used to be the old Post Office. And in the centre of this state-of-the-art development is a war memorial. The stone plaque lists the names of Post Office workers who were killed during the First and Second World Wars. Physical space carries memories. In the Met Quarter this memory has been implanted into a new development giving a link with the heritage that has been lost. Memory is a space between joy and sorrow. A safe enough space gives attention to memories and reminds people of their connection to their history and to their environment.

The sensibility underpinning this (planning) transformation includes the ability to tell, to listen to, and above all, make space for stories to be heard. We use stories in various ways to keep memory alive, to celebrate our history/identity; to derive lessons about how to act effectively; to inspire action; and as a tool of persuasion in policy debates. We uncover buried stories. We create new stories. We invent metaphors around which policy stories pivot. Stories, carefully told and carefully heard, have the potential to act as a bridge between ingrained habits and new futures. Stories can (usefully) disrupt habits of thought and action that control everyday life. The will to change has to come from an ability – a planner's ability and also a city user's ability – to imagine oneself in a different skin, a different story, a different place, and then desire this new self and place that one sees.[4]

Just in case we get carried away with visions of a utopia which could be 'safe enough' for everybody, we need to remember that physical spaces can carry significantly different memories for different people. Relatives of the Liverpool postal workers will visit the Met Quarter for different reasons than those people searching for expensive shoes. They will be searching for a name on a memorial rather than buying a name in a shop. Memories may be individual or collective, as in the District 6 museum in Cape Town where the exact location of the black residential area cleared during the apartheid years is being mapped. On the museum steps are the names of the roads that were bulldozed. Memory and naming are important keys in the process of '*sur vivre*'. One woman in the District 6 museum spoke of her distress that a certain road name was being changed (it is the current South African government's policy to rename places that have apartheid or colonial associations by using African names). The place in question was the site of a mass grave. 'How will we remember if the name is different?' she asked. The Afrikaans name of the place held important memories of this atrocity, and replacing it with the African name would displace the song line of memory. The memory is associated with the name. Safe enough spaces need to give room for memories and associations, even if they are painful.

Memories might be associated with individual sensations of light, smell, touch or sounds. Such associations can quickly transform a place into a safe or hostile environment depending on what they trigger. Not everyone finds the smell of coffee or newly baked bread appealing – for some it might bring flashbacks or panic attacks. The combination of an enclosed environment and sensory triggers can render a place unsafe for some, while others find it homely and welcoming. No one enters a space as a neutral observer; we all carry memories and terrors which can be sparked by our surroundings. The problem is that these will be different for everyone. This physical landscape in turn carries its own history so that in the same place some will feel they belong and others alienated. Joy and sorrow live together in the words and the silences of places.

This does not mean that we must all avoid what we consider to be positive influences in case they offend, but simply to say that, for a place to be 'safe enough', there must always be awareness of different memories – and the ability to exit.

### An eye to scale

Memories might be triggered by specifics in the local environment or by the sheer scale of the built environment. For instance, the vastness of Liverpool Anglican Cathedral may give some the anonymity of an open space, while others might just feel lost. We might find buildings intimidating in their size over against our physical bodies or we might sense a safety within their strong walls and spaciousness. Buildings with closed doors form barriers so that we are unable to see what they hold for us. Shopkeepers know that leaving their doors open even on the coldest day helps passers-by feel safe enough to browse. Being able to see beyond a threshold is a key factor for the process of '*sur vivre*'. We need to know what we are walking into, and the contents of buildings need to entice us beyond the threshold of our own fears. On the other hand, if we are inside a building with an open door it might enhance a sense of threat. Creating 'safe enough' spaces in the external, urban environment is complex, but we are challenged to consider this complexity creatively, listening particularly to the voices of those with insight into what makes a space safe enough to '*sur vivre*'. We are not simply people who live isolated lives without relation to other people or things but are accountable to each other. This depends on government policy and planning decisions as much as on the resilience of the individual human spirit. '*Sur vivre*' in relation to the built environment is a matter of justice and inclusion. It is the concern of everyone.

We need to remember that our physical environment is not a neutral space, because it engages with us in different ways and we will relate to it as a result of our varied memories, hidden stories and physical requirements. The outside world holds its own power, of scale and confinement, and enters an unspoken dialogue with our inner world. Buildings have a body language which provokes an atmosphere of fear or safety. Doors and thresholds have bearing on our well-being. Our physical surroundings have a physical power that can either confine or release us. Our safety is not an individual matter, it relates to the built environment and to government and planning choices that are made for us. 'Safe enough spaces' are those in which the collective and individual needs of people are held in balance with the power of the concrete world. '*Sur vivre*' is about justice, memory and community, but it is also about our internal emotional engagement with these outer spaces. It is the conversation between our inner and outer worlds that determines whether or not we have a safe enough environment in which to thrive, and this is what I want to consider next.

## Internal safe space

We need to recall that no place, either external or internal, is completely safe. The most confident people have vulnerabilities; this is part of what makes us human. We may be secure but none of us are completely 'together' and we all demonstrate these insecurities in one way or another. For people who have experienced trauma or abuse, that sense of inner safety may be missing altogether, leading to dissociation, amnesia, self-harm, multiple personalities, overwhelming terrors or some kind of disintegration of the self. None of us enters any environment as objective observers; we all carry experiences that influence the way we relate to our physical world. A place can only be safe enough when the inner world and the outer world find a resonance. So, finding safe enough spaces for stories to be heard and silences broken, for '*sur vivre*', needs an understanding of what makes for such a creative resonance. We all need spaces where it is safe enough to be unsafe.

What does it mean to be safe enough to be unsafe? Often we talk of vulnerability being a good human quality. We admire those who are vulnerable to others, who can be empathetic or let down their guard. But total vulnerability is not healthy, even in the most loving relationships. Total vulnerability is a relinquishing of all power and may leave us open to abuse. Every person needs an inner core of confidence and privacy before becoming resilient enough to be vulnerable. To be vulnerable in any positive sense means to relinquish some of the power of the self in relation to other people, but it does not mean relinquishing all power. It is in total vulnerability that abuse occurs, because power is taken in destructive ways and the result is damage and trauma.

The word 'trauma' comes from the Greek word 'to wound' or 'to pierce'. The body of someone who has experienced sexual abuse may have been literally penetrated or pierced, and the emotional bubble of safety that all children should expect is violated by abusers. This will probably lead to an ongoing feeling of violation, guilt, fear and insistent thoughts of being unable to cope. There can be disintegration of a sense of self, multiple selves or profound feelings of selflessness. Any notion of being an autonomous 'other' might be hard to grasp. Coping strategies are adopted by victims – the imagination of other worlds, of being someone else, of having other voices, of curling up like a possum, of the many manifestations of dissociative behaviour. Trauma is a violation of safety; it is the awful result of a place not being safe enough to be unsafe.

In her book, *Intimacy and Solitude,* Stephanie Dowrick talks of the twin human fears of being abandoned and being overwhelmed and posits that the autonomous management of self between these two fears is a natural human process. However, for those who have experienced abuse it becomes a huge challenge as traumatic experiences will have taken them beyond the bounds of autonomy into the realm of '*sous vivre*'.

A split between the way a person feels on the inside and the way they appear on the outside is usually maintained at considerable cost, with increasing feelings of meaninglessness and decreasing feelings of choice. Such a pattern of splitting is likely to be set in place when there has been a trauma which the child is not encouraged to recover from or speak about so that what the child is feeling on the inside is given no legitimacy of 'mattering' on the outside. Inevitably, then, inner and outer become unbearably divided.[5]

While Dowrick is speaking specifically about children at this point, this memory of abuse often continues into adulthood. Abuse steals this 'legitimacy to matter' from victims and leads to them being groomed and isolated on the one hand and smothered and violated on the other. Consequently many of the normative hallmarks of self are eroded, resulting in confusion, shame and guilt. In 1990 Chu and Dill looked at whether dissociative symptoms were specific to clients with a history of childhood abuse. Sixty-three per cent of the 98 hospitalized clients reported physical or sexual abuse and 83 per cent of clients scored significantly above the mean average for dissociative symptoms. Within that group there were significantly higher levels of dissociative symptoms seen in clients who had suffered either type of childhood abuse.[6]

Dissociation is one symptom of the fragmentation of personality, but others might be less obvious. All of us fear being overwhelmed, but for those who have suffered trauma or abuse this fear may mean that crossing any kind of threshold is too big a risk and entry into a group of strangers literally a step too far.

While this inner dialogue might be loud for those who have experienced trauma, it needs the perception of intuitive, attentive relationships for this to be heard by others. Any sense of making a safer space where it is possible to flourish has to be initiated by an engagement in safe enough relationships. So, what makes for a relationship in which it is safe enough to take risks? Some people who have experienced abuse will need the help of professional therapists to renegotiate a sense of inner resilience before any such relationship can be contemplated. However, an understanding of what makes for a safe enough relationship is not just for victims, but a basic human requirement in which all people can have the potential to flourish. Those who have experienced trauma or abuse may point to this need from their own experiences of violations, but it is to everyone's benefit to have an understanding of how relationships can be formed to be 'safe enough'. It is an issue not just for individuals but for the '*sur vivre*' of all communities, and indeed of the earth.

## Safe enough relationships

We must remind ourselves again that abuse is about the misuse of power, and '*sur vivre*' concerns a renegotiation of power in favour of those who have been silenced, the 'undoing of the binds'. This process of making a safer space might be an intentional process, as in the therapeutic counselling setting, or it might be within an organization such as a church or office, but most likely it will be within the to-and-fro of ordinary human exchange. There are a number of hallmarks of a safe enough relationship. Top of the list are that it is named, it is attentive and that it is possible to leave.

### Naming
In the story of the presentation of the baby Jesus in the Temple we note that everyone in the story has a name – Jesus, Mary, Joseph, Simeon and Anna. As in most human encounters, the exchange of names is a common courtesy, and this little group of strangers is no different. Not only do we hear that Anna has been a widow for years but we are also told her father's name and the tribe to which she belongs. The giving and receiving of names is a most intimate act, withholding our names a sign of resistance. In Liverpool, if we didn't feel safe enough to reveal our name to a stranger, we would retort, 'Who's asking anyway?!' Our names signal our identity, our personality and our individuality. We do not give names unless we know who is asking and what their intentions are in asking for our name. That is why oppressive regimes such as apartheid depersonalized the black and coloured people by referring them as 'kaffir', 'nigger' or 'boy'. At the Khulumani hearing we repeatedly heard people say, 'We were treated like dogs.' Giving and receiving names

opens up a safe enough space for a relationship to take another step. This may not be first name to first name. Some relationships name their participants by role – 'counsellor', 'client', 'parishioner', 'priest', 'daddy', 'teacher', 'boss'. If a relationship is named by role then it denotes a sense of responsibility and power. Exchanging our first names is a gesture of wanting to open up a relationship where the power is balanced, whereas defining a relationship by role is an indication of opening up a relationship where the differential of power is acknowledged.

A safe enough relationship is one where the power is named, either by giving and receiving personal names or by denoting the nature of a relationship by role: 'I am the teacher, you are the pupil.' If it is acknowledged that one person has authority over another then there is also a naming of responsibility for the other within agreed limits. When we enter into relationships with unequal power we are always open to being either abused or abusers. It is always the responsibility of the person with most power, not the one with the least, to ensure that abuse does not result. This is stressed in the report *Time for Action* which reinforces this message of responsibility for churches. Those in pastoral oversight are the ones responsible for maintaining proper boundaries – always. It is never the responsibility of the dependent or vulnerable party to ensure that abuse does not occur. Those in positions of trust also, by definition, have positions of responsibility. It is the duty of those with power not to abuse, not the duty of those with less power to prevent abuse. Once power differentials are named, then they must be owned. When the power is named, then responsibility comes with the naming, and safer relationships are free to develop.

If a safe enough relationship is one in which the power differentials are named and owned, it must carry a sense of each person being seen and heard. This might be a mutually beneficial encounter in which there is a to-and-fro of dialogue as friends meet over a cup of coffee, or it might be in a formal setting such as a job interview. The balance of power needs to be negotiated in such a way that there is no bullying or intimidation; this can be as simple as how many people are in the room, but also more subtly, allowing space for questions or uncertainties to be named and voiced. This may sound obvious, but it is astonishingly difficult to give the people in front of us undivided attention. If we go back to thinking about Anna and Simeon in the Temple it is easy to see how the significance of the moment could have passed them by. How many infants had that old couple seen come and go as they waited patiently for all those years believing in the fulfilment of the story of Israel? Yet, when Mary and Joseph appeared on the scene with another baby, they were totally transfixed. They not only saw the child, they understood the moment – a moment of history when time stood still.

### Attentiveness

Attention is more than just listening: it is an intuitive awareness both to what is being said and to what is not being said. As any musician will tell us, the gaps between the notes are as significant as the notes themselves. If we believe in a God who attends to the deepest silences of the human soul, then our listening to these silences becomes not just a courtesy but a vocation.

Person-centred therapists are not always known for their faith perspectives, but Mearns and Thorne have talked of 'the quality of presence' and feel there is a 'silence of communion where counsellor, client and the "something larger" are interconnected in a world where time stands still'.[7] This silence, Brian Thorne suggests, begins the rapport that initiates the process of healing and inner peace.

I experienced some of this communion, literally at Communion, in the Central Methodist Church in Johannesburg. Fifteen hundred Zimbabwean asylum-seekers sleep in the church at night and go out to look for work during the day. The church is full to bursting; people sleep in every corner and up the stairs. It is seen as a place of sanctuary after the desperate flight across the border. Invited by the bishop to participate in the Eucharist one evening, a colleague and I found ourselves distributing bread and wine to row after row of desperate people who had fled to search for safety and employment.

Indeed, this church building may seem anything but a safe space: the toilets are often broken, the lights fuse, and there is hostility from locals who are also searching for employment – but it is safe enough to be a temporary refuge. As I approached one woman who was bundled in what can only be described as rags, I was drawn to the look in her upturned face. Instead of putting out her hands to receive the bread, she passed me a bundle she was holding. The bundle was a baby. In the moment that I held that tiny, newborn infant, time seemed to stand still. As this child, born in destitution and most likely HIV-positive, lay cradled in the crook of my arm, I could have said with Simeon, 'This child will pierce your heart.' Yet, in the total attentiveness between myself and that troubled mother, in our silent understanding of our power differential in role and wealth and in the trust that enabled her to feel 'safe enough' to pass me that tiny child, we were indeed entering a world where something larger connected us within our humanity.

### Disengagement

Creative human relationships have space, a place of stillness between people which begins to embody a new trust. Such relationships also have movement. That is, they give the possibility of total attention but also of total disengagement. Even within long-term and committed monogamous partnerships there is the need to stand back, to take time alone, and to be free to walk away. That is not to say that we should not hold fast through the tough times and honour our commitments. What it does mean is that relationships should never be traps; they should hold and not bind. The to-and-fro of relationships within the attention of 'I' and 'Thou' helps us to understand that our inner world is under our control. We are able to maintain safer inner space in which we take responsibility for walking away from things that harm us. A safe enough space gives us the power to leave. In abusive relationships, such as the oppressive regime in Zimbabwe, or the grooming of a child by an abuser, this power is taken away. Creative relationships give us the choice to stay or leave. Being able to leave a relationship that could harm us is part of the unbinding and is an essential component of '*sur vivre*'.

## Covenant

In order to '*sur vivre*' we need to find, negotiate and create safe enough spaces. These spaces will not be completely safe but will have hallmarks of authenticity that begin to re-establish trust. These hallmarks are both external and internal and are expressed through our relationships with both the built environment and our neighbours. Relationships need to have an honest understanding of where the power lies and an implicit or explicit naming of responsibility. Such relationships need to be focused enough to embrace our full attention yet give freedom to leave. A safe enough relationship begins to unbind the things that have been bound, to give freedom to the physical body and to untie the tongue. It may be fleeting or long-term, between friends in an intimate setting or complete strangers walking along the same street. Safe enough spaces are a hallmark of '*sur vivre*'.

So, where is God in all this? Jesus says that he wants us to have life in all its fullness but seemingly takes on death as a victim of oppression. It seems that the God who desires that we '*sur vivre*' in order to speak and live, is often curiously silent. The Saviour who we understand as 'real presence' is noticeable by his 'real absence' and salvation is seemingly no longer a place of safety in which all are gathered, but an open relationship for us to choose or reject. These are some of the practical and theological dilemmas that my conversations have brought to light. They present sharp edges of a faith that can no longer slip into clichés about Jesus dying to save us all, without us asking, 'What are we saved from?' and 'What are we saved to become?'

I have continually asserted that abuse is about the misuse of power and to '*sur vivre*' is to emerge from underneath the story of oppression. What I have failed to say up to now is that love is also about power – the power to claim life, to live it and to transform what it means to be human. One of the tragedies of abuse is that it confuses the power of love and uses it to justify destruction rather than creation. This may be at a personal level when a father abuses a child or at a community or national level where a regime uses power, ostensibly for a common or greater good but actually at the expense of the powerless. It is also the case when short-term commercial enterprise defaces the natural environment or exploits poorer nations. Power itself is not wrong; it is the abuse of power that is wrong.

Let us consider now how we discover the creative power of God at the heart of God's self. Does it bear the same characteristics of 'safer space' that we have identified as hallmarks of creative human life? At first glance this seems a ridiculous question; surely the God of all power does not have to be safe – God is almost by definition unsafe. God is Creator, and creation is hostile, it relies on food chains where animals eat each other, where resources are scarce and species fight for dominance. Yet we are coming to realize that the earth is finite and the delicate web of creation has interdependency with mysterious depth and nuance. In Genesis we hear that the first human beings were not only made in God's image, but also given personal names. This naming of humanity denotes a particular relationship with God and has also brought us particular responsibilities. One of our first responsibilities was to give names to the creatures of the earth. God who gave us our names also gave us the power of naming and so we also have the responsibility that the naming brings. God knows our names because he also has responsibility for us, a responsibility for the loving use of power. In this way God seeks a safe enough relationship with humanity in order for us to be co-workers in creation. This naming denotes a covenant relationship in which power is also named and shared, and this covenant signifies a safe enough relationship between God and humankind within which life is possible.

This covenant relationship between God and humanity has become embodied in the person of Jesus. In the story of the presentation in the Temple, we hear of the baby Jesus being handed over into the arms of Simeon and Anna. Here the nameless God of 'I am' is presented into God's own story, by name – Jesus. In Luke 2.21 we read, 'On the eighth day, when it was time to circumcize him, he was named Jesus, the name the angel had given him before he had been conceived.' The presentation and naming of the baby Jesus signifies the continuing story of God, both bringing to fruition the old story and giving birth to a new way of being. Through Christ, God embodies God's self. In Jesus, God does not become powerless but demonstrates the creative power of love that comes about by living a faithful and authentic life in relationship with God. Jesus names this relationship 'Abba', and God names this relationship 'Son'. This naming signals the loving dynamic in the heart of God's self. God becomes incarnate, flesh and blood, but also remains distant. The space between Jesus and Father is a safe enough space for Jesus to live a fully human life attended to by the loving God of eternity.

Paradoxically, this divine attentiveness between Father and Jesus is both totally absorbing and totally freeing. We hear this in the early chapters of Luke as Jesus proclaims his 'manifesto' in the synagogue. Jesus declares that he has come to preach good news to the poor, proclaim freedom for the prisoners, recovery of sight to the blind, release for the oppressed and to proclaim the year of the Lord's favour. This is not just a declaration of social reorganization but an embodied message of a love that unbinds. Jesus, in person, is this message.

With this covenant relationship in mind, how is it that we quickly discover Christ as the crucified one, seemingly the victim of oppression and lies? I want to suggest that it is because the message of God is not about safety, but about safe enough space in which to live our lives differently. Through Jesus, God shifts the balance of power so that the strong will be weak, the poor will be rich, the hungry will be fed, and the downtrodden will be lifted up. This is not divine wishful thinking but a manifesto for '*sur vivre*'. Survival is not about avoiding suffering but about discovering within the 'story of underneath' a safe enough space in which to surface and be both transformed and transforming.

## Transformation

This transforming potential is not obligation but gift. Jesus chooses to be a victim, not because he is relinquishing power but because he is naming the power of love to live differently. His death and crucifixion are both eternal acts of solidarity and an earthed statement of the power of love. Here we see most starkly the power of God – given up within destruction but brought to life through love. Jesus did not simply die for our sake, and leave us stuck with atonement theology, but died and was raised so we can live. Paradoxically, the death of Jesus says to all victims, 'Live!'

Somewhat surprisingly, I am back with mission. The stories of those who '*sur vivre*' are not just peripheral to the life of society or the Church, they are stories that can transform our whole way of being. People who begin to surface from underneath stories of oppression and abuse, whether individual or national, show us a new way of claiming life in the here and now. They are the message, difficult and troubling though it is. I knew this as I held the small baby at the Communion rail of the Johannesburg Central Mission – a baby yet to be named – as a mother, in the simplest of human gestures, delivered her most precious and vulnerable child into my arms. I knew then something of what God was saying as he delivered his child into the arms of a troubled and struggling humanity. I also understood something of the moment between Anna and Simeon as Mary passed the baby Jesus into their arms. Here was an old story being born into a new and transformed story. Yes, there would be joy, but also anguish. This was the child to be pierced by the trauma of the inhumanity of humanity. This is something of what God means to '*sur vivre*' – it is both transformation and precarious, precious life.

In the township the women made a plan. If they heard, through their flimsy walls, that someone was being raped or abused they would all go outside with their cooking pots and long metal spoons. Together they would bang the pots so loudly that every person in the neighbourhood would know what was going on behind those closed doors. This is the solidarity of love, the power of transformation, the presentation, the naming, the beginning of creating safe enough space in the middle of it all. The women became the message.

I remember this as I stand in front of a coffin in a strange church. The autumn is damp and bone-aching. A group of old people sit in the front pew: Elsie's brother and sister, who had lived and continued to live with the silence and scars of abuse into their old age, still silent within a story that has not, and may never be, told. I know very little about this old lady whose funeral I am about to conduct, except for her name, Elsie, and that 'she suffered with her nerves'. Yet in the words and the silence that are around me I must say something that shows I have discerned a little of the underneath story. I say a silent and hasty prayer and start walking, 'I am the resurrection and the life, says the Lord . . .'

# Chapter 3

## Being Lost

All over the place, people are digging up things. As I write this, the news headlines concern an excavation at a children's home in Jersey that has seemingly concealed a site of ritual abuse for over half a century. In Rwanda and parts of South America there are the pits containing the remains of genocide victims. And in Liverpool we are in the process of digging up the city centre on the strength of being European Capital of Culture 2008. The process associated with survival, '*sur vivre*', entails excavation, raising things that '*sous vivre*'. Sometimes these things are dug up, sometimes they emerge over time. This process involves the bringing into the light of those occurrences that we are too ashamed to name or too remiss to remember. What emerges among the soiled and discarded rubbish are a lot of tiny fragments. Shards and oddments, disjointed, broken remnants, strange garbled histories. But, as the story surfaces, there can also be the piecing together of things, a reconstruction, a re-membering of broken bodies, histories and communities. That is why Laura and I are going to spend this Saturday morning underground, in the Williamson Tunnels, digging.

The Williamson Tunnels are one of those quirky mysteries of Liverpool. Joseph Williamson was thought to have arrived in the city as a child around 1780 and to have taken up employment at the tobacco and snuff firm of local businessman Richard Tate. Working his way up through the company, Williamson eventually made the ultimate career move by marrying the boss's daughter, Elizabeth, and the couple took up residence in Edge Hill, just a couple a miles out of the city centre. In time Williamson bought the Tate Company and became a man of considerable means, building houses for his workers with substantial facilities and gardens. Times changed, and men began returning from the Napoleonic wars without employment. Joseph Williamson continued to build, but this time his projects took him underground. The construction of arches and tunnels employed whole gangs of workers for seemingly no apparent reason other than to keep them off the streets. In time, a whole labyrinth of tunnels was dug, with amazing brick arches, sometimes three deep. It is thought that this was truly an act of philanthropy, helping struggling Liverpool families, although there was some suggestion that Williamson might have been making contingency plans for Armageddon! After their apprenticeships in Williamson's tunnels, many of the men went on to work on the new Liverpool–Manchester railway. After his death, the tunnels were used as places to dump refuse and were soon clogged up with the waste from a rapidly growing city. It is only recently that this extraordinary network has started to be excavated and Williamson's strange story has come to light again. Digging and surfacing are important themes in our discussion of what it means to 'sur vivre'. Stories are often physically or emotionally buried. The process of unearthing is crucial to our ability to piece things back together from those disjointed, lost fragments of the past. The physical act of digging is an immediate way to make connections with this process.

But before we disappear to an underground world I would like, first, to unearth a short story at the beginning of Luke's Gospel that often gets overlooked. It is buried between the birth narratives and what is commonly considered to be the 'manifesto' of the gospel preached by the adult Jesus in Chapter 4. Tucked at the end of Luke's second chapter is the story of Jesus as a young boy returning from celebrating the Passover in Jerusalem; or rather, not returning, because three days after the start of the return journey, and a frantic search, his parents discover the missing child sitting in the Temple asking the teachers questions. In what must be one of the most understated reprimands of all time, Mary asks, 'My son, why have you treated us like this? Your father and I have been anxiously searching for you' (Luke 2.41–52).

This story has probably been largely overlooked because it stands on its own, between the accounts of Jesus as a baby and the beginning of his adult ministry of preaching, teaching and healing. However, I want to claim it as a key text in Luke's account, in fact an embodied manifesto that comes before the later statement of intent that caused Jesus to be driven out of the synagogue and to the brink of the cliff. This little story reveals that Jesus began his ministry being lost, and as such it appears to be a precursor to much that Luke goes on to claim in the Gospel. The story signifies that God has come in Jesus to be lost among us. And this is borne up by the recurring theme of lostness throughout the subsequent chapters of Luke as we hear tell of the lost coin, the lost sheep, the lost son and finally the lost Saviour. In this way, the Gospel writer expresses the crucial place of the lost in the story of salvation. If we can begin to unpick this theme of being lost, then we might discover more clues as to how to make the movement from '*sous vivre*' to '*sur vivre*'.

Being lost is not simply about being separated from those who are supposed to be taking care of us in a physical sense. The loss associated with abuse breaks or confuses the relationship a child has with a primary carer, and results in a fragmentation of memories and disrupted patterns of trust. This carer is probably not physically absent but rather has power over a victim in such a way that the ordinary landmarks of growing up are lost. This loss can take a number of different paths. It may lead to a child being unsure of boundaries, not understanding the protocol of acceptable and unacceptable behaviour, or lead to a withdrawing from relationships into a dissociated, fragmented world. These things may not surface until much later, maybe well into adult life when a realization dawns that there are dark memories associated with childhood that have never surfaced. There may be an inability to sustain adult-to-adult relationships or a tendency to develop unhealthy attachments or destructive addictions.

Those who 'sous vivre' may have a sense that something is missing, that they are different from everyone else, that they never quite fit in; this is true of those who experience abuse as adults as much as for children. The secrets that they carry with them may hold physical terrors, they may give a feeling of pervading darkness, of having been buried or smothered. These things are carried in the mind and in the body. There may be scars or patterns of self-harm that embody the story. Stories manifest themselves in different ways – some may never be told with words. The depth of the silencing is most profound when the abuse happened in early childhood. When patterns of silence are deeply ingrained within a child's develop-ment, then it is particularly difficult to speak out about people who have held such significant power. Good parents tell you what is right and wrong, set appropriate physical and emotional boundaries and keep you safe enough to flourish. Therefore any sense of doubt is held against these assumptions, and victims tend to take the blame on themselves for what is happening – after all, little children learn that parents, by definition, cannot be wrong. This burden of guilt may go well into adult life, even when the rational person knows that abuse can never be the fault of a child. Guilt and silencing bury stories deep down.

These embedded stories are brought to the surface by a number of different types of excavations – gentle probing, explosive anger, long-term sifting or sudden revelation. It is much easier for us to understand what is going on in the emotional world of someone trying to 'sur vivre' if we engage with the physical process of unearthing. This is why Laura and I are off to the Williamson Tunnels on a wet Saturday morning in March to learn more about the connection between digging and becoming. Laura already knows considerably more about this than I do because she regularly spends days digging her allotment. This is the only allotment activ-ity she keeps exclusively to herself – it provides the mantra, the rhythm, the routine of her search for what it means to 'become'. I, on the other hand, live with a different kind of digging. Alongside people who struggle to articulate stories, who gather around the bread-making in my Liverpool community, who attend regular counselling sessions at Holy Rood House, the surfacing of stories involves a gentle process of delving, sifting, disclosure and discovery, and sometimes outbursts of rage or seemingly irrational behaviour.

Saturday reveals many things. First, my arrival through the cuttings and tunnels at Lime Street station reminds me that I often come up from under ground during my travels in the city. My routine journey from the suburbs is a subterranean one as the train dives under the business area of the city centre. There is in fact a lot of city below the surface, both physically and emotionally. There is a rather amusing sign in the city centre that says, 'Secret Underground Headquarters, this way', which refers to a Second World War operational base for the Battle of the Atlantic, complete with maps of submarine locations and a private phone booth for Churchill which was sealed up after the war and only discovered again recently. My mother has fond memories of Lewis's 'bargain basement' where she recalls trips from Chester after the war to hunt for affordable haberdashery. This subterranean aspect of the city centre is not simply physical, it is also emotional. There is a lot more to a city than what is visible to the naked eye. Alongside the articulate, employed and financially active occupants are the invisible classes, asylum-seekers, the homeless, those who skulk or hide or live in the shadows. So, the stories of a place are always multi-layered and the narratives are multi-faced and far deeper than the spin of the tourist brochures or development companies.

These lost stories are crucial to an understanding of identity because they exist beneath the crust of any dominant narrative. The subversive stories of a city are what give depth to the place, give the other side of perceived normalities and hold a mirror to the strata of power. They remind us that a city is not simply a construct but also an event in which ordinary people participate to form multi-stranded webs of meaning. Finding the lost stories of a place is not simply a quirky way to spend a Saturday afternoon but a physical and emotional engagement with identity. This became apparent as

Laura and I met the people who spend every weekend digging out the Williamson Tunnels.

## Digging down

Deep below the ground, in a scene that could have been lifted straight from *The Lord of the Rings*, two muddy men with shovels and pickaxes attacked the ground. It was as if they had appeared from the very bowels of the earth – we would not have been in the least surprised to have seen a troll passing by! These men were trying to find the third layer of the tunnel that stretches from a deserted stable yard in Edge Hill, an area on the edge of the city centre, to the existing excavation. They were intent on their work, unearthing the invisible deeper tunnel. They excavated with care; if they took up too many rocks they might have suddenly disappeared into the chasm below. On a ledge ten feet or so above their heads, two middle-aged men received the earth that was being slung up to them from the deeper excavation below. They stood precariously between the tunnel and the surface, ready to lob the loose debris upwards again to the two lads by the tunnel entrance. The lads scraped the earth together on a board, carefully picking out any artefacts that appeared to be of any interest – a piece of old chain, some discarded police tape, a bicycle frame, a patterned tile. Once it had been sifted, the soil was wheelbarrowed into a skip, ready for removal to a local landfill site. This discovery of fragments unearthed a lost narrative, bringing questions to the assumptions we hold about dominance and power.

The search for lost narrative, for discarded memory, for those things that we have considered worthless, critiques the layers of power around us. It is such an appraisal of power that enables us to consider those forces that lead to abusive behaviour. If we listen solely to dominant narratives, then we will overlook the silenced and the lost. Luke is at pains to inform us that it is the lost voices that are of foundational importance in the story of God. When he describes Jesus being lost in the Temple he is recounting much more than a transitional adolescent interval between childhood and adult life. To understand this story's significance we need to let it hold a mirror to the end of the Gospel. Decades later, it is the same Jesus that we discover returning to Jerusalem to face his death. The similarity between the story of the young, lost Jesus and the adult, crucified Jesus is remarkable. In both stories there is the turning back to Jerusalem, the mother who has searched longingly for her lost child standing at the foot of the cross, the young man who returned to the Temple to ask questions turning the tables on the *status quo*. The duration of three days in which everyone thinks Jesus must be dead is echoed in the three days he is in the tomb. This resonance is more than a coincidence. It seems that Luke is putting these two episodes like brackets at the beginning and end of his Gospel to indicate that the lostness of Jesus is foundational to our understanding of his life and death.

So, what does it mean to be lost? This is a deceptively simple question. It is a 'becoming' question and it is a relational question. We are lost in relation to something. This loss of relation might be a constructive thing, a time when we are going to wander in the wilderness and find our own identity. On the other hand, it can be totally destructive. The lostness of those who '*sous vivre*' can similarly be both. There may be a sense in which hardship leads us to a creative struggle to find the essence of our own souls. On the other hand, the cycles of deprivation and fragmentation may be such that we completely lose sight of ourselves. We are most likely to '*sur vivre*' if we know that someone is searching for us, that there is a longing for us to re-surface among those who realize we are missing. This longing is illustrated by Mary in the story of Jesus, and it is embodied by Jesus at the crucifixion. My journey of conversation with those who '*sur vivre*' has led me to believe that the crucifixion tells more a story of deepest longing than a story of sacrifice; I will return to this theme in later chapters.

Being lost is an experience deeper than losing our bearings or our landmarks. It is being in a place in which we have no idea that there might be any landmarks at all, where no one has shown us signposts, or where we are completely disorientated. This is the everyday experience of people who are experiencing trauma. Abuse is not just a blip in an otherwise normal life, it is a total disruption of normality. What is perceived to be normal is in fact destructive. It is this lack of ordinariness that is the biggest abuse, it leads to a total sense of disorientation in which the signals of normal life can no longer be trusted. Abuse leads to the dissolution of trust. If we lose all sense of what is trustworthy then we are in a place of total lostness, things no longer make sense, there is a confusion and fragmentation at every level of our being. Abuse is not simply something to be 'got over', it is rather an embodied experience – it forms us, just as the experience of being lost formed Jesus. The lostness of Jesus was not something he experienced and then forgot, but rather it was something he was able to refer to throughout his ministry alongside the lost people he encountered. Jesus came into being, into his own identity as the Christ, because he was lost. This, I believe, is why this story is so important.

## Digging up

The story of Jesus being lost, however, is not simply about being lost in isolation, it is also about the search to find that which has been lost. And Luke's message is not only about a child who goes missing, but rather about the search that begins to locate where that child might be found, which in turn begins to reveal his identity. It is this search that is crucial in the context of '*sur vivre*' for, in order for something to surface, there needs to be the realization that something or someone has gone missing, and this recognition initiates a process of unearthing. And this is why, all over the world, people are digging. They were digging in Rwanda after the genocide, in Chile when they searched for the 'disappeared', they dug in New Orleans after the devastating hurricane and in the rubble of the twin towers in the wake of 9/11. People dig for bones, for clues, for artefacts, for anything that remains of the people they have lost. They dig to recover their identity, their connection, their possessions and their loved ones. All over the world, people are digging – to uproot, to reveal, to disclose, and to claim. They dig into their memories, into their photographs, into their flashbacks, into the fog of half-forgotten experiences. They dig into their conscience, into their family history, into the subsoil of their collective stories. People dig, search, sweep, and peer, glean, gather, pick, dust, discern, forage and uproot. They do it with picks and shovels, with JCBs or with dustpans and brushes. They do it with the help of dolls or photos or conversations, in the company of counsellors, or psychotherapists or ministers or friends. It is the search of the survivors, those who endeavour to '*sur vivre*', who want to live on top of their stories rather than be overwhelmed by stories of oppression, people who long to surface and try to make sense of all that is lost under the rubble of disaster, abuse, environmental catastrophe or political misadventure. It is this digging that is the first sign of hope that individuals and communities are not content to be lost for ever, but that they are choosing to engage with the relational activity of '*sur vivre*'.

This is why the Khulumani counsellor takes time to sit with the women of the township and why the Holy Rood therapists give their own time to listen to people who have been abused. This is why there are people in South America joining demonstrations, holding above their heads the names of the women who die each week from domestic violence and why the families of District 6 in Cape Town document the exact location of their bulldozed houses. It is not simply so that justice can be done and restitution made, but rather that the submerged, silenced, buried stories of their life journeys can begin to be transformed. It is not the dominant narrative that is the source of gospel hope but rather the dawning of a new way of searching that is embodied by those around the Jesus who went missing. Jesus shows us the life-giving possibilities of 'being found'. He shows us how the buried stories of the lost can surface and be cherished as pearls of great price.

And this is why a group of men spend their Saturdays digging the Williamson Tunnels. On the surface it is a seemingly senseless act, but deep down they have a hunch that the city they want to inhabit is not defined by the bulldozers of the city centre but rather by the interaction of the story of the place, with the people of the place. In their bones they perceive that this city is their city, the place of their roots and of their embedded history. They belong to this soil, with all its crap, refuse, broken bits and friable sub-structure. This is why people dig – in order to know where they belong.

## Earthing and unearthing

The silent, testosterone-laden effort that Laura and I observed in the Williamson Tunnels reminded me of another occasion when I had seen men digging. It was at a West Indian funeral that I had taken some months ago in Toxteth, a suburb of Liverpool. The deceased woman had been young for a grandmother, probably in her late fifties and with a complex and troubled past but latterly with the hope brought about by her flourishing grandchildren and new-found relationship. In fact, six months before her death I had conducted her wedding ceremony. She had known that she was dying and had prepared as best she could with a mixture of tears, laughter and story-telling. Each day was a special day, and her family rallied around her and helped her to celebrate her last months. Although her death was expected, it was still a great loss. The whole community was grief-stricken and brought a resonant solidarity to the family that sustained them through the funeral arrangements. It was as the body was lowered into the deep gape of a grave that a moaning and singing came from the women as the men shouldered shovels and began to fill the hole. Shovelling and singing, returning a body to the soil, putting the story of a life back into the realms of eternity, letting grief flow with every strong push and shove, it was a physical expression of loss rather than a white, western, cerebral, clinical response. Grief came from deep down, from the bowels of the earth, and the lament was not of individuals but of the lostness of life and creativity and relationship. It was a tangible, physical grief.

And this welling-up of grief is not a sign of despair but an occasion of attentiveness by the God who 'groans in travail' with all creation. As any woman who gives birth knows, travail is not a polite process of controlled creativity. Rather it is the pushing out of the body, the severing of the intimacy of the womb and the gasping for air of new life. It has at its very heart the possibility of loss, of disaster, of collapse. Grief and birth, the lullaby and the lament, are not opposites.

In the Williamson Tunnels there is a bucket for artefacts, objects that have been discarded decades ago. Among the objects are some very intricate tiles from a Victorian washstand, a lemonade bottle, a broken chain, a bone. In some ways these artefacts are incidental to the job in hand, which is to excavate the tunnels. Laura and I were fascinated by them, not because they have any intrinsic worth, but because they are the means by which a story is being told. After a morning of pushing a wheelbarrow up a plank and tipping it into a skip, we are ready to stand back for a while and listen to these stories. At the same time as the men dug, groups of people were buying tickets to be taken around the tunnels by tour guides. They heard of how the engineer Stephenson, digging the new railway line into Liverpool, broke into one of Williamson's tunnels unexpectedly one day and, on finding a whole group of subterranean workers, decided that they must have broken into hell! The guides also explained the dilemma the project was having with Lottery funding and the collapse of a tunnel a week previously which had set back the possibility of meeting a deadline for grant payment. A group of ex-miners came past and began recalling their days in the colliery before its closure, and the lads at the top of the hole exchanged a progress report on their fitness programme. As stories were being dug up all around us, we too reflected on the digging that Laura was doing on her allotment, and the unearthing of stories that happens with the bakers at my church. There was something about the physical engagement with the soil and the dough and what surfaced with the diggers and bakers that brought other things to light. We described it as a sort of 'solidarity of unearthing'.

At Holy Rood House, the art therapist works with a group of residents in the art studio. The task that she has set is to paint a picture using colour and shape rather than an accurate depiction. One young woman draws bars and then prints two bright orange handprints onto the surface. When the picture dried, mysteriously the hands appeared to be behind the bars rather than in front of them. From this physical depiction of what was going on deep within her came an upwelling of sound, not really words but a gasping for air. Something deep within was beginning to surface; it was born of a long, maybe lifelong, process of discovery from the dark recesses of her buried past. But this sound was also a sound that signified a gasping for life, a birthing coming from the grief. She will need a good midwife within this process, but the sound is a sound of hope.

Unlike many people who '*sous vivre*', Jesus was not lost to himself. He presumably knew exactly where he was. The story has a sense of a lad forgetting time, of being intent upon something more important, being distracted by a quest for truth, rather than a complete fragmentation of the psyche. For Jesus, growing up in a loving and attentive family, there is no doubt that there are those who would return to find him: he had a mother who stored up his story in her heart and a father who also turned on his heel to find where he had gone. The story may be very different for those who are totally disorientated by abuse, trauma and loss, for whom there may be no sense of homecoming or that anyone is searching, for whom the notion of someone searching for them might in itself be fraught with terror. They may not know that they are longed for in a creative rather than a destructive way, that there are people willing to spend anxious time searching for them or that there might be a new way of living with attentiveness and care. So, not only are people digging all over the place, but people are digging in different ways. And it is this interaction between the lost and the searchers that is both the imperative of the gospel and the imperative for '*sur vivre*'. People search gently with counsellors, they search clinically with physicians, they search rigorously with lawyers, they sift, excavate

\*          \*          \*

and probe, they puzzle, struggle and fight to remember, they search alone or in company, they scrape the surface layers away until they can distinguish a semblance of truth. The process of '*sur vivre*' is about engaging with this losing and finding process, this digging up. And this is a matter of hard graft, because no word, no definition and no account will ever do justice to the truth.

'Survivor' itself is such a difficult word. It defines those who have pulled through in relation to those who have not. It may seem to define someone by their victimization rather than their fight for freedom. It is necessary to remember that people who 'survive' are so much more than survivors, they are nuanced, complex, contradictory, passionate human beings. Survival is a relative term, a term in which life is rated in relation to death. It is a value-laden word with both positive and negative connotations. It can also be a guilt-laden word, a word that leaves people labelled as survivors and asking the question, 'Why me, when others suffer so much more or have never surfaced to tell the story?' Who is this God of love who apparently saves some and not others?

Adrienne Rich, in her poem 'Through Corrialatos: Under Rolls of Cloud', wonders how we can know what it means to survive; she says it is not possible: 'Until you take the mirrors and turn them outward and read your own face in their outraged light?'[1] This struggle for language, the defining of one against another, is the reason why I am using the counterpoint of '*sur vivre*' and '*sous vivre*'. I am aiming to see this digging, this unearthing as a to-and-fro process, by which stories emerge, collapse, are sifted and sorted, reach a conclusion and begin again.

## Turning the mirrors outwards

What is this process by which we can 'take the mirrors and turn them outward' as the poem suggests? If we return to the story of Jesus as recounted by St Luke, we see revealed a divine imperative for the lost, not in the sense that they can become as one of the powerful, but rather that they are worth more than the 99 who are already found. Jesus chooses the lost, chooses to be lost among the lost, and chooses to be lost to those who love him because he sees among the lost the possibility of being alive in a different way. This way is a way of treasuring those things that a dominant regime overlooks, it is a way that leads to connection with Samaritans, with lepers, with prostitutes and with women who bleed. It is a chosen connection, not through some sort of superficial altruism but because it is within these encounters that a possibility of transformation can be realized. The message of the Gospel is that those who are considered of no worth, the last in the queue, the unacceptable, the ritually unclean, are not simply included but actually the point of the story. Jesus is lost, because of the lost. It is the lost that matter most.

This Jesus way is not simply a nice story about a man who went about doing good things. It is a story that is going to turn the tables on the values of a society, indeed of the world, not just for a few months until he can be forgotten, but for all time. Jesus takes the mirrors and turns them outwards on every deep-seated belief and value system. The Jesus in the Temple and on the cross, lost for three days to those who love him most, is living out this 'holding of the mirrors' and showing us the face of 'outraged light'.

There is a hermit who lives in the woods in a Swedish-style barn made by fellow monks. He lives alone now except when he is host to visitors. A group of socially aware city-centre clergy went to spend some time with him for a quiet day, amidst the push of the 'Make Poverty History' campaign, and a conversation ensued about the cancellation of debt and fair trade legislation. We were in mid-self-righteous flow when he gently challenged us. We were speaking as if poverty could be eradicated, that no one should be poor in this day and age, that what we longed for was equality and justice for all. In his opinion we had not quite got to grips with the phrase 'Make Poverty History': after all, Jesus reminded us that the poor would always be with us. He went on, kindly but firmly, that we needed to understand that rather than eradicating poverty we needed to unearth an understanding of history that comes through poverty.

The poor have stories of value, of struggle, of resilience and of strength, stories of the human and divine spirit that throw a light on everything we assume is important. This was not to say that we should sink into complacency about the rich man in his castle and the poor man at his gate, or cease to be outraged by the inequalities of class or caste. Rather, the hermit challenged us, if we could become people who could attend to the stories of the poor, really listen, and really understand, we would have a transformed, deeper, richer comprehension of the message of the Gospel. Eradicating poverty was, he said, just another sort of colonialism, where the power remained with the powerful and the dominant narrative prevailed. Hearing the history of poverty was a much more challenging task; it was a call to transformation, of seeing the world the other way round. I think this is the essence of what Jesus was embodying in his life among the lost. I think this is what it means to take the mirror and hold it outwards. I think this is what is meant by 'outraged light'.

The truth the hermit points us to is also true for our understanding of those who '*sous vivre*' and '*sur vivre*'. The listening process, with which we are called to engage, is not so that poor abused people can feel better about themselves, but rather so that the transformative potential of lost stories can transform all of us. To use another metaphor, it is rather like a seed bank.

When I was studying agriculture in the mid-1970s the aim of the agronomist was to develop strains of crops that could provide uniform quality, size and vigour. Plant-breeding institutes were in the business of developing strains of cereals and potatoes that could easily be harvested by machinery, could provide a uniform product for the supermarket and be resistant to pests. These dominant strains were marketed wholesale; farmers no longer saved their own seeds from previous years but entered the competitive arena of commercial farming. Yield was everything.

Since that time, the assumptions of dominant intensive agriculture have been called into question. We have realized the stupidity of uprooting hedges, extending fields to roadsides and engaging in monocultures that require the application of expensive herbicides. Some of the longer-stalked wheat varieties, for example, are seemingly less likely to cause allergic reactions and the seeds of these varieties have been rediscovered in old thatched roofs. Seed banks have become an invaluable resource, a place where the old varieties are rediscovered. There is growing understanding that diversity is preferable to uniformity within a healthy ecosystem. Cross-breeds can give a different kind of vigour to progeny, and settling for less quantity can sometimes result in a greater quality and variety of products. The seed bank is the source of this potential; those things that were once rejected are now seen to hold the secret for a new understanding. The genetic code holds a hidden story of unborn possibilities for '*sur vivre*' – it holds the mirror outwards.

And in the city centre, it is this kind of engagement with diversity that is also the key to the dialogue between '*sous vivre*' and '*sur vivre*'. It is not sufficient to engage with the poor in order to meet government targets on social inclusion. It is within the stories of the poorest that we begin to see the germ of a new understanding that gives the possibility of transformation for all.

I am writing this during Holy Week. Yesterday I came off the train at Liverpool Central Station and made my way up the ramp onto Bold Street, ready for my usual hug from John the *Big Issue* vendor. But although John was there, he was not in any mood to be happy, in fact he was crying. A couple of addicts had been giving him grief for a few weeks and he told me, in his few words of English, that they had just been past, grabbed him and spat in his face. I invited him to come back to our 'bread church' for a coffee – John often comes for lunch – while he collected himself. We began to make our way back up the street when the two abusive people returned and again began to spit and shout at both of us. I stood my ground between them, and in the end they retreated. But not for long, because as we made a second attempt to get up the street they reappeared, threatening and cursing. So, John and I stepped into the entrance of HMV and called for the police.

I tell this story, not to highlight the foul behaviour of some people who are victims of their own addictions, nor to turn John into some kind of martyr or hero: rather, to point out that this is the diversity within which we all need to live. Diversity is not a comfortable word, it is real and challenging. We are neither called to be local heroes nor to walk by on the other side. We are nudged by the imperative of the gospel to attend to what is going on, to the complexity of the stories that are being told around us. We cannot simply live on the surface, attend to the dominant narratives, to the vigorous strains, to the articulate and vocal. We must be mindful of the undercurrents, the sub-plot, the things that lie buried or in the dark, to the fragmented people whose lives are in bits, to the disappeared, to the lost. And this is not so that 'they' can become like 'us' but so that 'we' can learn what it might mean to '*sur vivre*' on the same street, in the same world, as the invisible, silenced people of the same earth.

## Surfacing

All over the world people are digging, searching, wanting to discover the remains of a past that has disappeared. Because, if we can discover the silent, invisible stories of the earth there is some possibility that we will find hope for our future – our future together, the future of everyone. This is no small matter; it is the stuff of life and death.

Being lost is relational. Those who are lost are not only missing to themselves, but to those who search for them. 'Disappearance' is not an objective description of inanimate objects but a description of the loss, anguish and terror of those who search. Jesus was not lost to himself but to those who went back to find him, the coin to the woman, the sheep to the shepherd, the prodigal to the father. The lostness of Christ is not an individualistic, subjective narrative but reveals the relationship between the undiscovered and the seeker. That is why, all over the world, people are digging. They have a relationship with that which is lost. This relationship, between the lost and those who search, is the beginning of a transformative process, an embodied demonstration that, despite everything, all is not yet lost. A message that it folly to some and foolishness to others is the beginning of the alternative narrative of hope, a narrative of discovery that will transcend the immediate story of lostness.

The relationship between the lost and the searcher is not the unhealthy attachment of an abusive and coercive relationship which stalks the abused into the shadows of their own terror, neither is it the detachment of the mystic who is seeking to be free from all earthed desires – although this is not intended as a criticism of mysticism. The searching that the incarnate Jesus speaks about is the longing expressed by the silent and longing God, who attends to those who have become invisible to the world. It is a demonstration of the possibility of a creative attachment, one in which there is a pattern of holding and releasing, a place where power is not used for any destructive end but only for the intention of mutual flourishing and life.

To return to our conversation concerning mission, we see that it is essential for the Church to offer places where the lost are safe enough to ask questions, where there are life-giving rather than coercive patterns of attachment, and where the longing for the lost is a relational endeavour rather than a coercive drive to fill the pews. In the story of the lost Jesus, the young man was discovered in the to-and-fro of questions in the Temple. Despite the struggle with those in authority, it is remarkable that the Temple elders were prepared to give time to a 12-year-old who chose to sit down with them and ask questions about life and faith. How different from many contemporary faith communities that are probably the last place on earth where it feels safe enough to bring questions of human and divine significance or to find people who are prepared to live with the troublesome search for meaning, the dialogue between the lost and the searchers, the relationship of '*sur vivre*'. I have come to see that the most effective 'tool of evangelism' is the ability to sit down with people and have questioning conversations. This, after all, was where Jesus began his ministry.

Last year, a group of people from the bread church, 'Somewhere Else', travelled to South America. We were all survivors in some way – of abuse, relationship breakdown, bereavement or homelessness. We flew to Santiago and then north to part of Chile that used to be Peru, Alto Hospicio.

Alto Hospicio is a town perched on the edge of the Atacama Desert, between the Andes and the sea. Two Methodist Mission partners work there, Revd Alison Facey and Chris Esdaile. Chris is director of a project working alongside women experiencing domestic violence – there is at least one death a week through domestic abuse in Chile. Alison is minister of a church in the middle of a housing area which has only recently been given a water supply and street lighting. In Alison's church our small group of 'survivors' from Liverpool gathered with a similar gathering of people from the church for an evening of sharing stories. Our Spanish was negligible and our generous hosts acted as translators. Slowly, courageously, as one woman began to talk of her experience of domestic violence, one of our group nodded a sign that this had also happened to them. A younger person shared her experience of coming out as gay and another person spoke of their endurance of childhood abuse. With a group of people in a strange land, across the difficulties and differences of culture and language, stories were born among us. These stories were difficult to tell and hard to hear, but on a dark night in a strange country we were able to hold them for a while in a simple, safe place, and connect with each other's humanity. I believe that mission is not about one side converting another to their point of view, but in the moments when God breaks open conversations and calls us all through our pain and injury into a new community of trust and attentiveness.

## Chapter 4

# Boundaries

We are walking along a crack. At first a hairline, but now widening slightly and taking on a jagged course along the floor. My friend walks on the other side but playfully steps across to be with me. A few steps further on, we have to separate again because a young man's girlfriend is taking a photo of his foot down the space. We skirt around the couple and are now separated again across the deepening crack. The artist Doris Salcedo formed a fracture in the floor of the Turbine Hall at the Tate Modern, the crack is called 'Shibboleth'. The exhibit programme tells us that a shibboleth is a word used as a test for detecting people from another district or country by their pronunciation: a word or sound very difficult for foreigners to pronounce correctly. It is therefore a way of separating one people from another. The word refers back to an incident in the book of Judges where the Ephraimites, attempting to flee across the river Jordan, were stopped by their enemy the Gileadites. Their inability to say the 'sh' sound marked them out as strangers and they were duly captured and executed.

A shibboleth is a token of power: the power to judge, refuse and kill.[1]

My friend and I find ourselves standing at the end of the exhibition, either side of a line that stretches beyond a reflective wall and on into infinity. The crack, which started as an imperceptible line between us, is now as deep as the foundations of the building and appears to go on for ever.

I want to consider boundaries, how we set them and how we transcend them, but as I begin to explore the divisions between people that lead to 'sous vivre' I am brought up short by 'shibboleth', a line of division that goes down to our very foundations. Doris Salcedo refers, through her work, to the postmodern world's legacy of racism that has cracked modernity to its foundations. As a generation we do not have to take total responsibility for such divisiveness. The word 'shibboleth' can be traced back before the time of the Judges. Since humanity stopped wandering and started enclosing territory, the desire to exclude through difference has been the hallmark of settled, territorial communities. How then can we begin to negotiate boundaries in a creative way when they are so often used to segregate, discriminate, persecute and exclude? How do we begin to understand 'salvation' when it is so often used as a weapon of exclusion in order to secure a faith identity? What are life-giving borders, and how do we move from walls and barriers to open up wide enough, safe enough spaces for people to flourish, 'sur vivre' and become themselves?

In order to explore these enormous questions I go to a short story in the eighteenth chapter of Luke's Gospel (Luke 17.11) in which we find Jesus walking back to Jerusalem on the border between Samaria and Galilee. Jesus walks on the edge between those who worship the one God of Israel on the mountain in Jerusalem and those who believed that Mount Gerezim was the appointed place of sacrifice. Samaritans were considered unclean, unsuitable company and imposters. It is on this edge that a voice is heard – actually ten distant voices – all calling for attention. Jesus bumps into ten lepers, in a marginal place of hostility and exclusion. Samaritans and Jews, we are told, did not keep company. Lepers were excluded from both groupings, consigned to live in places that kept others safe from their contamination. This is where we find Jesus; he does not ask for 'shibboleth' – on the contrary, he lets the lepers approach him.

## The double bind

In our understanding of '*sur vivre*' any discussion of edges, bound-aries and borders brings us to another bind. Abuse leads to a sense of lost identity, violation, isolation and silencing. It also leads to a feeling of overwhelming dependency, powerful bonds of obligation and fear. Abusers render people both totally beholden and totally isolated. Paradoxically, lack of boundaried behaviour does not result in freedom but to a double bind of dependency and isolation. We may describe this isolation as exclusion but we should not use the word too glibly because the concept of exclusion has been used recently to prop up the political agenda of 'inclusion'. I want to con-sider the factors that lead to exclusion and go on to ponder how these can be changed. I am working towards the notion that the opposite of exclusion is not inclusion but rather the acceptance of diversity. Let us first consider what is meant by exclusion.

Speaking from the context of the Serbian/Croatian conflict in the former Yugoslavia, Professor Miroslav Volf skilfully outlines the factors that lead to exclusion. He sees that there are two starting points, first when someone becomes totally distant and claims ulti-mate power over someone else, and second when someone fails to distinguish between different people, reducing them to a voiceless, undifferentiated mass. The following is a rather lengthy quotation from his book *Exclusion and Embrace* but I sense it offers an impor-tant critique of the 'double bind' of exclusion.

What then is exclusion? In a preliminary and rather schematic way one can point to two interrelated aspects of exclusion, the one that transgresses against 'binding' and the other that transgresses against 'separating'. First, exclusion can entail cutting of the bonds that connect, taking oneself out of the pattern of interdependence and placing oneself in a position of sovereign independence. The other then emerges either as an enemy that must be pushed away from the self and driven out of its space or a nonentity – a superfluous being – that can be disregarded and abandoned. Second, exclusion can entail erasure of separation, not recognizing the other as someone who in his or her otherness belongs to the pattern of inter-dependence. The other then emerges as an inferior being who must either be assimilated by being made like the self or be subjugated to the self. Exclusion takes place when the violence of expulsion, assimilation, or subjugation and the indifference of abandonment replace the dynamics of taking in and keeping out as well as the mutuality of giving and receiving.[2]

Volf speaks of exclusion happening for two polarized reasons: the first, where a powerful person sets himself or herself up to be superior to another and renders them invisible and their needs irrelevant; the second, where a person sets himself or herself up to be exactly the same as another – in this case there ceases to be a differentiated 'other' and they become invisible and their needs irrelevant. This rings true. If I consider the situation of a woman who has been systematically and ritually abused, I can see that she is made victim in both of the ways that Volf describes. Her abuser has assumed a role of all-powerful persuasion in which her needs have become irrelevant to his lust for domination and satisfaction. At the same time, however, she has been lost in a sea of 'sameness' because she is just one member of a family in which the cycles of abuse are endemic. She believes that her experience is 'just how it is' and so fails to speak out for fear of destruction on the one hand and ridicule on the other.

With this person who has experienced abuse in mind, I sense that it would be useful in our discussion of '*sur vivre*' to turn Volf's analysis of exclusion around so that we see this double bind clearly from a victim's point of view. Here is my paraphrase of his quota-tion from the perspective of the abused:

What then is exclusion? We can point to two interrelated aspects of exclusion. First, exclusion is being made invisible by someone who assumes superior power over us. We are rendered irrelevant and of no consequence. We are therefore pushed to the edges of society or relationship to a place of silence, worthlessness and loneliness. Second, it can mean being owned or manipulated by someone who assumes power over us to such an extent that we lose any sense of autonomy, are not seen as differentiated beings and it feels impossible that our distinct voices will be heard.

Looking at Volf's analysis of exclusion this way round reveals something of the double bind of the victim. It is not that there are two types of exclusion, one from an oppressor who assumes sovereign power over us and another from a different oppressor who fails to see us as distinctly different. Written from a victim's point of view, Volf's two aspects of exclusion combine into a double bind of silencing and isolation because we can see that victims are both irrelevant *and* overwhelmed *at the same time*. That is, they are simultaneously completely related to 'the other' but also rendered totally irrelevant by 'the other'. A victim's experience of exclusion is not dependent on the psyche of the one who excludes but rather on how they experience abuse. Regardless of the motives of the abuser, a victim experiences this double bind of exclusion; this is why it renders them feeling unable to make easy changes. Whatever choice they make, they will be compounded in one cycle or another, of isolation or of ridicule, rendering them simultaneously more dependent and more isolated.

I have laboured this point because any understanding of '*sur vivre*' should not underestimate the impact of this double bind. In order to not be a victim of either oppression or invisibility, there needs to be a strategy for negotiating real boundaries that simultaneously protect both autonomy and just relationship. One of the first steps towards '*sur vivre*' lies in reversing the structures of power in such a way that boundaries become liberating rather than constraining. In a series of paradoxes, the binding that comes from abusive relationships leads to an unhealthy interdependence, exclusion from which would lead to apparent freedom. However, such 'freedom' can actually be exclusion. The path to '*sur vivre*' comes through neither total interdependence nor though total exclusion but through the positioning of boundaries that allow the dynamic between exclusion and autonomy to be unbound. This placing of different boundaries is the responsibility of the powerful; but in the case of abuse, this responsibility is not taken. The abused person is unable to unbind herself from the knot of victimization without the solidarity of others. These 'others in solidarity' need to be prepared to enter into the bind and release it on behalf of the victim. Victims rarely move out of the cycles of abuse on their own but rather need the support, insight and understanding of those who 'stand in solidarity'. These individuals are not people who are prepared to be always available or totally subject to a victim's needs but rather those who can respond by drawing appropriate boundaries for the suppressed stories to surface: '. . . exclusion is different from drawing and maintaining boundaries . . . boundaries are part of the creative process of differentiation. For without boundaries there would be no discrete identities, and without discrete identities there could be no relation to the other.'[3] Who are these 'others in solidarity' if the network of distrust and alienation has been all-pervading? Who will change the boundaries and who will stand in the gap between the abused and the abuser as a trustworthy 'other'? This requires an intentional strategy of trust-building that operates with clear boundaries, a process that takes time and loving attention, brought about by people who act as midwives to the story, such as the Khulumani counsellors. This is a painstaking process of attentiveness, courage and transformation.

Writing from the context of post-apartheid South Africa, the feminist theologian Denise Ackermann critiques Volf's argument this way:

> Mirolsav Volf suggests, 'keeping out' is bad and 'taking in' is good. Is this necessarily right? Total inclusion collapses all borders. When this happens, we lose our sense of what criteria to use in deciding between repressive identities and those that

are good and affirming. We cannot be all things to all people. Yet, maintaining strict borders can be an act of exclusion and oppression . . . on the one hand I see borders as a healthy and necessary strategy to make space for the nurture and growth of what is the unique self of every person, on the other hand, if borders serve to exclude me from real conversation and the possibility of change, they are not healthy.[4]

The establishment of healthy borders by 'others in solidarity', boundaries where there is space for an unbinding of the double bind of oppressions, marks the beginning of the process of transformation that we have described in our understanding of *'sur vivre'*. It relies on people being able to stand in the gap between different people and open up a space for the knots of suppression to be unbound.

## Together in difference

We can see an example of this unbinding if we return to St Luke's Gospel and the story of Jesus with the ten lepers on the border between Samaria and Galilee. These men not only had leprosy but they also lived on the outskirts of a village between two hostile regions. At least one of them was a Samaritan; we assume the others were Jews. As they see Jesus approaching they begin to shout, 'Jesus, Master, have pity on us.' The men are caught in the double bind of oppression as they live between two states, neither of which welcomes them because of their illness. They have been overlooked by those in power as irrelevant and pushed to the edge of society. They are both completely isolated from their own communities and yet totally bound by those same communities to remain in the company of fellow lepers. They have been defined as 'lepers', a term that negates any difference between them; they are both Jew and Samaritan, yet the term 'lepers' fails to recognize the distinctiveness of their humanity and experience. The state boundaries that have defined 'Samaria' and 'Galilee' and the community concerns that have labelled 'leper' and 'clean' have placed them in this double bind, powerless and excluded.

How does Jesus address this? First, in an act of solidarity with the oppressed he goes to the place of 'no belonging', the border between the two regions. In stepping into this border area between Samaria and Galilee he is entering a dangerous area of solidarity with the displaced people he finds there. Although he may not have intended to encounter a group of lepers as he walks in this edge country, we note that he hears them calling to him from a distance. They address him as 'Master', and immediately place him in a position of power. Jesus is attentive not only to their shouting but also to what they are voicing; Jesus does far more than see with his eyes, he also understands what he is seeing. He notices that they are different but he does not ask for a shibboleth; he observes that they are strangers, but nevertheless enters into a conversation. This dialogue is such that it is safe enough for them to express their need. This 'seeing' is an intuitive understanding of otherness, in which those who are powerless are given power. Jesus embodies this return of power as he instructs the lepers to 'Go and show yourselves to the priests' and 'as they went they were cleansed'. This is a healing, not just of the body, but a reinstatement, a restoration of the displaced person. In this engagement Jesus enables them to enter a process of returning to themselves; in other words, before they are healed they are given back the power.

It is intriguing to speculate which priests Jesus sent these people to. We imagine that it was the priests in Jerusalem, in which case there was a scandalous crossing of borders. Not only do unclean men arrive to be cleansed, but they include a Samaritan, a foreigner. Similarly, if Jesus sent the lepers to Samaria, the Jews were entering foreign territory and challenging the exclusion of generations. Either way, Jesus gave these people permission to cross a societal border in order to seek reinstatement, to claim the power for their own destiny and to be free of the double bind of their exclusions.

As Denise Ackermann has suggested, the frontiers are not dis-solved, they are re-configured, so those who are excluded are reinstated. It is not that Jesus has dissolved the border between Samaria and Galilee, but rather passage across this boundary has been made possible through giving back the power in the process of restitution and healing. He has, in effect, widened the border from a line to a zone. In this zone there is a possibility for human engagement and transformation; it is not simply that Jesus and the lepers have seen each other, but also that the priests have seen a new challenge to their assumptions. Power has shifted in favour of the excluded, and the notion of 'the other' now has a human face. In this wider border zone there is the chance of a new way of relating. This new way brings with it the possibility of transformation, not just for those on the edge but for political and social reconfiguring. Without such engagement with diversity this possibility is lost in a melée of sameness or is open to becoming victim to the next oppression.

> The differences between us, and the ways in which we deal with the question of difference, shape our identities. By 'difference' (often called 'otherness') I mean the fact that we are not alike, that while humanity is marvellously diverse, we find difference problematic, often threatening or even alienating, and we don't always live easily or well with it. For example, we often speak of 'the other' in a way that mistakenly assumes she is just like me when, in fact, she is not like me at all; or conversely, we perceive 'otherness' as totally foreign and are then surprised to find that we share common interests or feelings. To speak of otherness is also to be open to otherness within myself, to the possibility of a foreigner within my own unconscious self. To speak of difference and otherness is to speak of gender, of race and class, of poverty and justice, of human sexuality, of history and tradition. To speak of difference is to acknowledge difference even in one's own family.[5]

If we are to discover a new way of relating, it is not simply a matter of including the excluded, but rather of learning to live with the diversity that is around us and within us. The political rhetoric of inclusion still tends to keep the power with the powerful. Those already 'in' are able to incorporate the outsider into their power structures, but this does not change or critique the structures. The inclusion agenda may lead to a society with more 'in' and fewer on the edges, but it also leads to policies of zero tolerance for the street homeless, shopping malls policed by security guards and a monochrome environment based on retail, commerce and financial prosperity at the expense of the vulnerable. This is not the gospel of Jesus. In contrast to the modern desire for progress and uniformity, the gospel as lived by Jesus shows that the opposite of exclusion is not the rhetoric of inclusion but rather the honouring of diversity, to live with those who are different and to find strategies for autonomy while maintaining community. In this way the gospel agenda is far deeper and more demanding than is implied by inclusion. '*Sur vivre*' requires an intentional embracing of diversity and a struggle with what it means to be 'together in difference'.

## Others in solidarity

What does it actually mean to 'live together in difference'? What kinds of relationships enhance our chances of '*sur vivre*'? Who are 'others in solidarity' and how do they unbind the oppressed, give sight to the blind and set the captives free? I would like to share four stories. One is a story of personal transformation. One reflects on a city in the process of redevelopment. One looks at a community standing as 'others in solidarity', and the last one considers how someone who has experienced victimization and trauma begins to flourish.

Earlier in this book I spoke of Dave who stands at our door, who chats to me in the morning as I fumble for my keys. Dave would tell me who had arrived already, who had come and gone, who had been asking for me, and what the news and football scores were – all before I went inside. He also had a fund of jokes, some of which I understood! Last week Dave wasn't at his usual post and we gathered from the *Big Issue* office that he had been taken into hospital having had a massive stroke. On Wednesday, Dave died. We learned that he had just had his sixtieth birthday, that he had worked most of his life at a local company, had had his fair share of struggles, and during the time we knew him was either living on a friend's floor, in the YMCA, or latterly under a bush outside the Anglican Cathedral. We also discovered that he had a family in Liverpool and was a Roman Catholic. His funeral was to be a requiem mass at a local church.

Being a female minister in the middle of Liverpool is not always easy. This city has had deep sectarian roots. Within living memory, children of Protestant and Catholic families were not allowed to play together in the same street, and I am occasionally referred to as 'Father'! There have been times when I have looked after someone pastorally, or been involved ecumenically, or been invited to be involved in a service in which I have experienced a very deep exclusion. Most poignantly and painfully, this sadness has been felt in being excluded from receiving bread and wine at the Roman Catholic Mass. To me, such exclusion is achingly counter-gospel, theologically inexcusable and rude. It has often made me cry. I was steeling myself for this at Dave's funeral.

As it happened, the local priest was very open to my involvement in the service. I sat at the front of the church and looked out at an interesting selection of people who had somehow been touched by Dave's life. Along with people from our 'Somewhere Else' bread-making community, I could see his remaining brothers and sisters, some friends from his workplace, the Sisters of Mercy who take in and feed the street homeless, someone who lives in the Cathedral precinct, the poets who share our building, a number of wandering city men, the women from the bookshop next door, the staff from the *Big Issue* office, and others I did not recognize. It was an interesting gathering of humanity.

The priest and I stood together at the front of the church while he broke bread and said the words of the Mass. When it came to the distribution, some came forward, others remained seated. As is the custom, I did not receive. Instead of feeling my usual anger and hurt at being excluded from the feast most central to my faith, curiously I felt something else. Yes, sadness and a profound sense that this should not be so, but also a realization that my place, as a Methodist, as a Protestant, is not to look wistfully at the Catholic Church and desire a place. Rather, my role is with the excluded, and that is where I choose to be. I would rather stand in solidarity with the excluded and be without bread than be included without those people I love so much from the margins.

To return to Volf's analysis of exclusion, I usually feel overlooked in such a context because I sense that those who hold power consider me to be irrelevant and not really authentic in my faith and role. I desire the Roman Catholic Church to acknowledge that we are all the same under God. Here is the double bind by which we render each other invisible because we are not the same, our differences are significant and part of our identity. Methodists and Roman Catholics will not find transformation by fudging the boundaries between us, either by saying that these differences do not matter or by holding out that one or other of us is totally correct. We will only transform our relationship by being ourselves, as 'others in solidarity', by finding a wider border zone where we can meet within our difference and find that we are all changed. As at Dave's funeral, the believers, the wanderers, the devout and the disassociated gathered together, distinctly different but glimpsing a shared humanity, so the gospel of Jesus gives the possibility of a new way, a way of unbinding in which each is released to be different but each is also free to be heard.

The second reflection also comes from Liverpool – Capital of Culture for 2008. The Culture Company was given the job of preparation for this status as, 'The World in One City'. In the past few years, Liverpool has undergone a process of huge re-configuration of the city centre, a multi-million pound retail development, with the consequent doubling of rents and property prices. As I write, a gay and lesbian Christian group was moved from their usual gathering place and an Alcoholics Anonymous group displaced because their meeting rooms were needed for 'Capital of Culture'. I am left asking, 'Whose culture?' I have talked a lot so far about the birth of individual stories, how they can be unbound and brought to a safe enough space in which to be heard. In contrast to individual stories, 'culture' is the story of a place and the peoples of a place, and as such has a multitude of strands, nuances, depths, resonances and memories. Tim Gorringe defines culture as 'the web of significance we spin for ourselves'.[6] Local culture, as opposed to 'high culture', is perhaps best understood as this union of people and place and the emergence of a depth of story. In such a way a particular place and time-bound web of significance can emerge.

As I read it, Gorringe makes his argument from the point of view of the powerful. The powerful are in a position to spin their own webs of significance. Victims, however, do not spin their own webs: they are trapped in double binds by other people's webs of exclusion. Gorringe's call to discover the 'meeting point of people, place and story' implies the possibility of a safe enough space which enables different people to see and hear each other. Gorringe asks, 'To what freedom do we aspire?', and in the middle of the destruction that the city has undergone, the answer seems to be, 'We desire the freedom of conformity.' But again, if we turn the argument around to the perspective of the poorest, we are presumptuous to talk of 'aspirations' at all.

The encounter between Jesus and the lepers is not a meeting of conformity: it is one that pushes all involved, a mix of the ordinary and the unacceptable, the empowered and the struggling, the religious and the outcast, from religion. In the days of Jesus, lepers did not aspire to anything – they were in the business of '*sous vivre*'. It seems significant that one of the most threatened places within Liverpool's new development is St John's Market, a place where a truly diverse mix of stallholders, asylum-seekers and bargain hunters mingles. There are a number of stalls on the market run by immigrant families: a Polish woman sells traditional food, an Iranian family share news of their extended family in their own language, a Zimbabwean stallholder takes time to sit with other Africans who have come looking for a bargain.

Alberto Magnaghi in his book *Urban Village* calls for transformative processes to be realized as the city opens up 'practical spaces for social action and imagination'. His vision for a diverse and locally sustainable city environment pushes us towards a reversal of the processes of silencing and conformity.[7] The market is just one such place of social action and imagination as opposed to the globally uniform retail outlets which sport names such as Armani, Hugo Boss and Timberland – names that are the same the world over. Does 'Capital of Culture' mean that Liverpool must espouse the same culture as Manchester and London, or could there be the possibility of reclaiming the stories of the invisible that have been made invisible by the heroic stories?[8] In the Met Quarter the heroic stories and upmarket retail outlets suppress the invisible stories of the homeless, the elderly and the simply tired, like Dave. Seats become 'display items' and the doors are locked at night.

'Living together in difference' is a challenge in this world of multinationals and image-makers when our aspirations are so often driven by the pressure to attend to the heroic narrative, to our desire for conformity and success. Widening the borderlands of the city means taking a radical step of imagination in which it is possible to honour the stories of diverse communities. It means having the courage to give proper space to those who dwell on the edge and in creative places of encounter, such as the market stalls in St John's Market, that not only provide goods for migrant communities at affordable prices but give opportunities to talk in a mother tongue with people a long way from home. In this way the stories from underneath begin to surface, a rich cultural diversity is brought to the city centre, we begin to understand that our 'web of significance' is not owned by multinationals, but as part of our ordinary and precious experience of being radically different human beings, of urban '*sur vivre*'.

Tim Gorringe reminds his readers that culture is organic – about human flourishing rather than exponential growth, and this is a pertinent reminder in the face of Liverpool's development as 'Capital of Culture' in which we are seeing a huge and speedy reconfiguration of the city centre. The underlying assumptions of the development agenda are predicated on commercial competition within national and global markets. Yet, human flourishing is not the same as economic development. The stories underneath are tender, nuanced and contradictory. Structural growth of the city centre pulls money away from inner-city areas in which houses and shops are boarded up and communities divided by new roads. Organic growth is not a mad, competitive rush to be like our commercial rivals – Liverpool wanting to be like Manchester, Manchester like London – rather, a call to be ourselves. Such growth requires a confident sense of identity, of imagination, and of integration within a region. To my mind it implies a call to understand our own particular culture, our particular 'web of significance', the unique and many stories of the place rather than the construction of flimsy illusions of prosperity.

My third reflection returns to Santiago, where our small group of 'survivors' was invited to meet with a church that makes bread each week to feed the children and homeless people in the neighbourhood. Bread-making is close to the heart of the Liverpool travellers but we were nervous to meet with a group of 'experts' who were working within their own context and understanding as well as in a language we were unable to speak. We were greeted warmly, and spent a little while talking rather formally about our churches with the help of a translator. Then, one very old lady, who couldn't have been more than four feet tall, took us gently by the hand and led us to the kitchen. Here were flour, oil, yeast and salt ready to be mixed in big bowls. We were handed aprons, hats, spoons and mixing bowls. And there, in the middle of a kitchen in the heart of a huge South American city, thousands of miles from home and without a common language, people from Liverpool and Santiago made bread together with respect, honour and a great deal of laughter. Later, we went together to share it with the many street homeless who gather on the steps of the city centre church. No one could have built or constructed such an amazing experience; it literally grew from a willingness to meet as human beings to share what we had in common and to learn from our mutual vulnerability. In this way the basics of life are transformed into something far beyond any plan or design.

At Holy Rood House there is an art exhibition. Someone who has suffered the most appalling ritual abuse has been painting. The pictures are challenging, full of colour and distress, but they also have poems and insights from her journey. It has taken a great deal of courage for her to put them on the wall. We have hung them secretly without anyone knowing who the artist is, she does not think they are very good. Through the courage of this one individual woman the walls of this room are becoming a creative place of imagination. We are opening up a place of conversation, letting the light into a dark place, showing something of what it means to '*sur vivre*'. The therapeutic counselling engagement that has been going on confidentially, week by week, has brought us all to a new place. We are being given insight into the resilience of the human spirit within it all. On this creative boundary a new sense of human relatedness is being born. Some are challenged by the pictures, for others there is a painful realization of their own hidden stories. For those of us who are engaged with church communities, we are challenged to recognize our own complicity in the language we use and other unhelpful manifestations of power. This borderland is a place of flourishing, not just for people who have experienced abuse, but for everybody. This is what happens when we learn to be creative about borders, giving power to the voiceless and imagining stories into the light. This woman may never know the impact she has had, but her journey through trauma is becoming an agent of transformation for herself and for others. I want to name this as a Godly thing.

Jesus remains on the border between Samaria and Galilee while the lepers go to the priest and are reinstated into their own community. But one man returns – a Samaritan, a foreigner. This man, full of thanksgiving, returns to the border to find Jesus. He becomes the focus of thankfulness within this story of healing, not just for himself but for the borderlands. He becomes the point of the story. It is in his returning to the place of exclusion as a new person that we hear this gospel story being changed from one of healing to one of surprising transformation. Luke so often wants to tell us that it is the most unlikely, the most hurt, the most excluded, and the poorest who are the centre of the gospel. He claims that those who bring a different story to the surface, who '*sur vivre*', begin to show a new way of becoming human at the edge of conventional experience and understanding. As the thankful Samaritan comes back to Jesus, together they make the border zone of exclusion the very heart of God's mission. Mission stems from those who open up safe enough borders, wide enough borders, peaceful enough borders, for stories to be honoured, for people to return to life. It is not so much about what we preach, but about who we are becoming, and what we attend to, that makes the difference as we inhabit the edge places with God.

Laura and I sit on the allotment. In a quirky kind of way we are a 'community in solidarity' as she talks about her art project, I talk about my writing. I discuss the border between Zimbabwe and South Africa, she talks about her neighbours. It seems that there have been complaints about the plants of her diverse and wild allotment growing over the wall into neighbouring plots. We smile and nod. Such disputes are all too common in our small island, a place where personal territory is delineated by fences and hedges. We talk about the word 'becoming'. What does it mean? I remember my father-in-law, a simple and kindly Cornishman. He used to describe people as 'becoming'. He meant that they were beautiful, but not in any conventional pretty way, more a handsomeness born out of an inner quality. We smile at this old-fashioned word, yet there is also some truth here. 'Becoming' is not simply a useful word to describe progress, but rather a quality of life. A city such as Liverpool could be 'becoming' if it unhooked itself from the modern concept of progress and began to find its own qualities of beauty, individuality and uniqueness in the stories of the people of the city streets. A person who has experienced abuse is 'becoming' as she paints her story in vivid colours, finds words to describe her experiences, challenges an interaction with her viewers and begins to reclaim her life. There is a new quality to her engagement, a sense of inner beauty that is born despite it all. A country can be 'becoming' as it learns to manage its boundaries, claim its stories, and be people that stand in solidarity with those on the margins. A leper is 'becoming' as he returns to the enemy who has healed him in thankfulness. The gospel is 'becoming' as it sees the beauty of a stranger and the widening of the borders between estranged people that give a new way of relating. Laura and I are 'becoming' as we discover within our conversation what it means to '*sur vivre*', to live our stories in a different way.

In the book, *Wrestling and Resting*,[9] Jim Cotter writes that salvation means 'wide open spaces of freedom'. For anyone such as myself who has done battle over the years with earnest Christians asking me if I have been 'saved', this brings a whole new perspective to the answer! These 'wide open spaces' are not un-boundaried licence to do anything at all, neither are they fenced-off territories of religious certainty, but rather places that are safe enough to explore what it means to be a human being under the gaze of God. Contrary to the jargon of cultish Christianity, this concept of salvation begins to bring new possibilities of a space in which to dance, explore, question and play with the edges of life and faith. It talks of living our own story under the gaze of an all-seeing, all-loving and attentive God, a saviour who calls us back to the edge places in his company, a spirit that delights in diversity and sees possibility in difference. This is the gospel that Luke describes as he notes the Samaritan, healed and returning, thankful, bemused and transformed. This is not only our salvation but the salvation of the earth, a new way of relating that views the edges as essential places of new possibility.

I ask Laura what she did about the neighbours. 'I was angry,' she said honestly, 'what difference did it make that a few stray weeds grew across a wall? Then I realized that it looked different from their side of the fence, so I tried not to over-react. I cut down the offending branches and, when I had harvested all the plums from the fruit tree, and the raspberries and tomatoes, I made jam and chutney and took a jar to everyone on the other side of the fence – even the ones who weren't complaining!'

# Chapter 5

# Breaking the Power

As many as were able flew out to my niece's wedding in South Africa. We couldn't miss witnessing such an important occasion. It mattered to be there. My mother is now too old and frail; living in a residential care home, she rarely remembers who or where she is. The arrangements for the wedding passed her by as we tried to connect her with the excitement of it all. We learned later that while we were away she would often jump to her feet and set off to join us. According to another lady in her lounge, Mum's expeditions to 'South Africa' often ended up in the hairdressing salon!

When we all got home there was a plan for a celebration in Liverpool. The newly married couple were to don their wedding outfits and cut a cake with friends and family who couldn't make it to the original ceremony. Mum's confusion meant that my brother felt that it was unwise for her to come through to Liverpool. She is prone to fall, is often bewildered and the journey seemed precarious. Anyway, she would be unlikely to remember the occasion.

On the Thursday before the celebrations I was suddenly troubled by the image of Mum in her care home while we, as family, rejoiced together. She has always been the centre of such events and, like a mother hen, loves to see her brood gathered around her. It suddenly seemed very wrong not to make some attempt to get her there. So, when the Saturday evening came, Mum was duly togged up in her best clothes, hair done and jewellery selected. With a lot of help we managed to get her in and out of cars, drove slowly and sedately up the motorway, and made a grand entrance to the party. She brightened visibly, declared it to be 'great fun' and was delightfully bemused to see members of her family who she clearly recognized but whose names she couldn't quite place.

By the time she was back in the care home she had forgotten all about it, went to bed happy and to my knowledge has not mentioned it since. She has, however, stopped setting off for 'South Africa'!

Has my mother forgotten the party? Was it worthwhile taking her? Well, at one level she wasn't really ever in a position to remember it. Her mind has an incapacity to hold on to recent facts although she has a canny ability to recall every last detail of being at school. What I came to realize from this sudden impulse to collect the old lady was that it is not so much remembering that matters, as *being there*. Sometimes our bodies are witnesses in a way that our minds cannot rationalize. What we see with our eyes and hear with our ears holds a deep, embodied memory, whether we consciously remember it or not. 'There,' said my brother, as Mum posed for photos with the bride and groom, 'now you have seen all your granddaughters married.' Our bodies carry memories that connect us to our 'webs of meaning'. Our bodies and our identities are intimately linked.

People who have experienced trauma or abuse are often encouraged to 'forgive and forget' as if this was a mere act of willpower. But this injunction overlooks the fact that bodies as well as minds carry memories, both good and bad, and we cannot forget our bodies. Remembering gives us identity, both in relation to others but also in our bodily selves. We carry both emotional and physical scars and they mark us with stories that may be crushing or defiant. Similarly, our bodies are the site of our resilience as much as our minds. My mother is kept alive both by willpower and a strong constitution. We are embodied beings, earthed and real. The ways in which our bodies forget and remember make us who we are as much as our mental ability. Our bodies hold power, the power of resistance and solidarity; those who suffer abuse have this bodily power undermined and so to '*sur vivre*' implies the restoration of the body so that, even with its scars, it can begin to tell another story.

I am reminded of a trip I took to Germany just after the fall of the Berlin Wall in 1989. I was staying with a family who had formerly been living in East Berlin. To my incredulity they showed me maps in which the roads stopped at the Wall, and the forbidden part of their city was denoted by a blank page. With great delight they also showed me a book of photographs in which they as a family were seen among the crowd holding candles at a night vigil of solidarity and prayer for transformation. It not only mattered that their world had been transformed into a new, wonderful and troubling reality, but it also mattered that their bodies had been physically present at the process. In their struggle they had put their bodies where their hopes were.

I have been skirting around the issue of whether Jesus was in fact a victim in the same way as someone who has experienced abuse is a victim. I have been resisting this issue because it is so laden with doctrinal baggage. However, if we are to consider the power of the body to remember, we must consider the body of Christ and how it was used and abused. So, we cannot avoid the question any further. 'Was Jesus a victim, and what implication does this have for our understanding of remembering, forgetting and "*sur vivre*"?'

## Was Jesus a victim?

In many ways a victim of either national or personal abuse does not have choices. Abuse happens to them, they are trapped, silenced, damaged, even killed by others who have taken away any sense of their autonomy or self-worth, they are made into objects. This is not the case with Jesus. Jesus did not need to go to Jerusalem, was not obliged to stay silent before Pilate as many are silenced by abusers, he could have been less provocative to those with authority over him. His death may have been inevitable, but was it unavoidable?

Was the death of Jesus the natural consequence of the life of Jesus? I do not believe that it was all a predetermined reality put in place for God to prove a point. Jesus may have been declared innocent by a thief on an adjoining cross, but he was surely provocative; no one goes around flouting laws, being rude to authorities and turning tables in temples, however justifiably, without sensing there might be repercussions. In many ways it seems that Jesus brought his death upon himself, unlike many people who have innocently suffered abuse. He remained the subject of his own story. The victimization of Jesus needs some unscrambling from the victimization of a child abused by a father, a mother whose son is shot while he was playing in the street, or a baby stillborn because a security guard kicked a pregnant woman in the stomach.

The portrayal and honouring of Christ as a sacrificial victim is troubling and dangerous for those experiencing abuse. Feminist theologians have long resisted the motif, seeing it as a device put in place by the narrative of Kyriarchy, that is, the lordship of Christ within a dominant, patriarchal tradition. From this perspective, Elisabeth Schüssler Fiorenza writes in *In Memory of Her* of the need to reconnect with the gospel, the *basileia vision*, which emphasizes the needs of the nameless ones, those who fail to be heard, and the lost. She acknowledges that women's life and faith stories can struggle to be heard. It is often hard to find an authentic route to flourishing that finds the inner strength to overcome persistent messages of self-negation. That is, women should become subjects of their own stories, learn to value their bodies and minds, and resist the loss of self that is espoused by the dominant narratives of religion.

> As a feminist vision the *basileia* vision of Jesus calls all women, without exception to wholeness and selfhood, as well as to solidarity with those women who are the impoverished, the maimed and outcasts of our society and church. It knows of the deadly violence such vision and commitment will encounter, it enables us not to despair or to relinquish the struggle in the face of such violence. It empowers us to walk

upright, freed from the double oppression of societal and religious sexism and prejudice.[1]

For this reason some feminists have named the sin of women not as pride, but lack of self-worth. Maybe, but any sense of worth may have been robbed by experiences of trauma and abuse. We cannot make too much of ourselves if we do not know ourselves and value our souls and bodies as unique and important expressions of God's love. This is not just a gender issue. In order to live as full human beings, people of both genders and all sexual orientations need to be enabled to break the bonds of self-negation and enforced submission. Called into question is the motif of the sacrificial lamb going silently to slaughter through substitution doctrines of the atonement. Through the writing of Elisabeth Fiorenza and other feminists this dominant narrative has been challenged, there has been a fresh call to find the hidden voices, the ones unnamed in the story, those who live underneath, '*sous vivre*'. This is true not only for women, but for all those who struggle as victims of power beyond their control.

The varying theological reflections offered by feminists and womanists alike emphasize the fact that different people have different life-course trajectories and therefore different journeys through faith. Those who are born into power are called through Christ to begin the process of self-giving love, the setting aside of pride and self-centred living, as Christ did, through the radical act of following the way of suffering. On the contrary, those who are born into powerlessness, whose lives have been violated, subsumed and stolen, those who '*sous vivre*', are called to find freedom, safe enough space in which to claim life and flourish. They are not obliged to submit to repressive, self-denying demands but to find strength and authenticity through the bringing to light of the truth. In other words, the imperative of faith is different, depending on one's position in relation to the forces that oppress.

The radical act of love embodied by the life and death of Jesus demonstrates that God's attention to the lost has caused God to put his body where his hope is; he has chosen to be lost, so that the lost will be found. This is not the action of a hapless victim but a consequence of the divine choice for covenant love – true love that longs for the beloved to be all they are intended to become. Here, at the end of Luke's Gospel, we see the mirror held to the story we discussed earlier, where the young Jesus is lost in Jerusalem. Mary, who hunted high and low for her son and found him asking questions with the elders in the Temple, now stands at the foot of the cross where her son is raised as a challenge to all authority and powers. The cross stands as the question mark between heaven and earth both as a sign of judgement to perpetrators and a sign of solidarity to the lost. The lost coin, the lost sheep, the outcast, the leper and the violated are held high, for all time, by the lost son.

In this way the cross of Christ stands in silent contradiction to the silencers. On the one hand, the cross judges perpetrators and challenges them to live in a different way. On the other hand, the same cross offers a way to '*sur vivre*' by which those who have experienced abuse are offered not judgement but a radical act of love. Through the cross, God through Christ makes a choice to be profoundly present in the silence, absence and violation that are experienced by so many people, and in this way the 'power over' another is transformed into 'strength within'. Rather than the crucifixion of Christ being the end of the story or salvation, it is the pivot on which the story turns. Perpetrators are judged, the abused are upheld. Their wounds become the stigmata by which they are marked, but, as for the risen Christ, these wounds are transformed into the hallmarks of identity and life. Jesus was not defeated by the cross, he was raised. This is the way of Jesus.

### Remembering the body

This is dangerous territory. It is very easy to slip into language that denies the trauma and destruction of abuse. We need to remind ourselves that abuse is not a theory, it is a bodily reality. At Holy Rood House, counsellors hear of stories that may defy belief. A mother who let into a house a series of men with the intention of sexually abusing her daughter, a man ritually abused in a seminary, a young woman forced to abort her baby. Such experiences are so traumatic that they often lead to dissociative behaviours. These behaviours are designed by the human body and mind to blot out experiences that are too painful to recall, they are a defence mechanism. Pushing things into another world, another personality, another frame of reference, may be a way in which a person gets through the immediacy of abuses. Although the will to prevail is crucial, such traumatic forgetting is not a route to flourishing, it often leads to cycles of self-negation, self-harm and bleakness. The process of putting into order, re-making and re-membering those things that have been dis-membered, fragmented and shattered is the beginning of the process of finding strength within; 'sur vivre' is both a mental and a bodily labour.

We need to remind ourselves that abuse is robbery with violence and will never be 'got over'. It is not sufficient to say, 'Christ was crucified with you and therefore you are not alone'. For someone who has experienced abuse there needs to be a process of strengthening from within, a slow, painful journey into self-belief, a realization that life has worth. Ironically, apparently negative coping mechanisms such as comfort eating, self-harm and addictions may initially be beneficial to the process. They are used as moments of control in a world of chaos. In similar ways political prisoners have smuggled out subversive texts, communicated with adjoining detainees or tried to escape. Ostensibly these ploys could lead to further damage but are truly acts of subversion and taking power. The beginning of bodily 'sur vivre' is defiance in the face of victimization, the decision to live in the face of death. Rather than the language of forgiving and forgetting, those who seek to 'sur vivre' need the vocabulary of resilience, solidarity and resistance. Instead of the agenda of vulnerability so often offered by the dominant narratives of faith in the light of the death of Jesus, they need the agenda of determination, inner strength and defiant hope.

## Resilience, forgiving and forgetting?

The *Concise Oxford Dictionary* defines resilience as the ability of an object 'to recoil or spring back into shape after bending, stretching, or being compressed', or in the case of a person, 'to be able to withstand or recover quickly from difficult conditions'.[2] It comes from the Latin *'resilire'* which means 'to leap back'. In his work with young people leaving care, Mike Stein offers the following definition of resilience:

> The quality that enables some (young) people to find fulfilment in their lives despite their disadvantaged backgrounds, the problems or adversity they may have undergone or the pressures they may experience, resilience is about overcoming the odds, coping and recovery. But it is only relative to different risk experiences – relative resistance as distinct from invulnerability.[3]

From another context and another time, Julian of Norwich wrote:

> God did not say you will not be troubled,
> you will not be belaboured,
> you will not be disquieted
> *But God said, 'You will not be overcome'.*[4]

What is this resilience that gives the possibility of *'sur vivre'* and the belief that we will not be overcome? If I consider my mother in her hazy and forgetful world, or the family who stood with candles by the Berlin Wall, or the woman at the Khulumani hearing who followed the police truck containing her children and kept vigil outside the police station, or the person who painted pictures of her sexual abuse and named the perpetrator, then I see people living in a different way. It is not denial or wishful thinking, it does not negate or reinstate the past, and it is not just about 'bouncing back' and not being vulnerable. These remarkable people are making radical, costly statements naming the possibility of transformation. They are remembering, in their scarred and fragile bodies, holding fast to the possibility that things can be different. Despite the inevitability that abuse is not 'got over', there will be an ongoing struggle to live with the events of the past; the determination to '*sur vivre*' is a way of life, not a way of death. Survivors are saying, through their physical resilience and resistance, that ultimately and finally they will not be overcome. This is the way of Jesus; it is the stuff of resurrection.

So, what of forgiving and forgetting? What a problem these words present to people who have suffered abuse! Who dares speak of such things in the light of personal and political atrocities? I hesitate – we should all hesitate – before the enormity of such significant words.

Laura and I meet at her allotment in the first week of January. The ground that she has dug is bare and empty, apart from the old beetroot which are crisp with frost. This year she has decided to lay the plots out slightly differently, the triangular configuration of last year was complex and the paths hard to discern. With a ball of string and some long canes we begin to mark out the edges of the new patches, Laura measuring the distance between beds by her standard foot lengths. Once the borders are marked, we begin the trampling up and down, puddling the dug soil down into distinguishable pathways. We go backwards and forwards over the same ground until we can distinguish which is the soil for this year's planting and what constitutes the way to travel between the seeding areas. To and fro over the same ground, until last year's paths begin to disappear and we can see the way marked by our footsteps, until we can see the beds that will flourish with next season's seedlings.

There is no mention in the Bible of forgetting, except in relation to remembering. 'Can a mother forget the baby at her breast . . . ?' (Isaiah 49.15). The question is rhetorical: could Mary forget Jesus, could the Khulumani women forget their children in prison, could the raped woman forget her aborted baby? Of course not! No one has the right to bid another person to forget, forgetting is a consequence of brain degeneration, illness or trauma. In forgetting we lose our web of relatedness, our sense of identity and the possibility to begin to change our future in the light of the past. No one can command another person to forget, not least ourselves. So, to disobey my own injunction, let's forget about forgetting!

But surely forgiving and forgetting are inextricably linked? How can we forgive if we are always recollecting bad memories or reliving abuses through dreams and flashbacks? Mary Grey writes that 'Forgiveness is a word based on "letting go" for the sake of moving on, away from bitterness and hatred to a new way of being.'[5] I feel I want to articulate this slightly differently. I believe forgiveness is a process by which it is possible to break the bonds of abuse and find the strength within that will help us to become transformed, free human beings within our community, the 'wide open spaces of freedom' in which we can slowly and painstakingly find ourselves. In this I want to affirm that this 'letting go' is a process which is for the benefit of the one who has been abused rather than for the perpetrator. Forgiveness, then, is not a retrospective reinterpretation of the past but a way of remembering in such a way that the future will be transformed. Restoration and reconciliation may be one possible outcome of such a process, but they are not just another obligation on the victim. True life cannot be claimed unless these unhealthy bonds of obligation are broken. It is not the primary work of the victim to make amends or to reinstate a perpetrator. The victim's job is to put blame where blame is due. This implies removing blame from where it is held falsely, namely with the one who has been abused, and seeing that what has happened to them is neither their fault nor their duty to heal for another who has acted maliciously towards them.

## Putting blame where blame is due

'For-give' has both a sense of future and a sense of gift. So what is the nature of the process by which the gift is received? The very nature of abuse confuses this discernment process, and heaps blame and guilt on victims. Somehow what has happened must be their fault, they must have led somebody on, appeared overly vulnerable or somehow confused a relationship. This sense of guilt is often reinforced by family, friends or colleagues. Victims often have strong feelings of affection and loyalty towards the people who have abused them. They might even feel that they love them. They are therefore inclined to take blame on their own shoulders and assume that they are worthless or flawed. This belief can be reinforced by theological motifs of justifiable suffering and self-denial. It is important in some ways, then, to make a distinction between tragedy and malice. That is, it is necessary to distinguish between the things that simply happen to us and are endured and those things that are deliberate acts of malicious intent. In the former we need strategies of integration, in the latter the language of outrage.

Putting blame where blame is due is a matter of putting responsibility with the perpetrator rather than with the abused. Let us be quite clear about this. If a person has authority over another through rank, status, age or a duty of care, then that person is *always* responsible for maintaining appropriate boundaries. A 15-year-old girl can stand in the street scantily dressed and with a sign round her neck saying 'Rape me' but an adult who touches that child is *always* the guilty party.

Putting blame where blame is due often comes through remembering and naming what has happened. As in the Khulumani process, this telling is to a person or community that 'bears witness' to the story. This bearing witness is a key role of friends, counsellors and mental health-care professionals. 'Bearing witness' is an interesting phrase: it implies the holding up of the person telling the story. It acknowledges that the account may well be inaccurate, hazy, confused, but is prepared to hold fast in the telling, without judgement or reproach. As Mary and the disciples bore witness to the death of Jesus, those who have borne witness throughout the ages will experience the most profound sense of helplessness, anger and grief. Those who bear witness are not called, themselves, to be victims, they are responsible for finding appropriate support and supervision outside the listening process – not simply for them-selves but also so that they do not bring secondary abuses through inappropriate boundary setting. Bearing witness, like all bearing, is a heavy load and takes its toll on all who stand alongside victims in relationships of solidarity.

As individuals and communities bear witness to what is being told, these relationships of solidarity begin to form a new frame of reference. The story begins to open up, the truth told, secrets unearthed. Those who bear witness are called to react as human beings, to indicate what is out of the ordinary, to demonstrate a degree of appropriate outrage. For many people who have experi-enced abuse, the knowledge that their experiences are out of the ordinary is a key to remembering in a different way. There is some-thing to compare the experience with – not all life is abuse, not all relationships are destructive, and there can be an unconditional, positive regard and acceptance, despite everything. The listening process is key to a person's ability to forgive himself or herself; that is, to release themself from the bonds of false guilt and to come to believe they have strength and significance.

## Tragedy and malice

The Dutch theologian, Ruard Ganzevoort, working specifically with male survivors of sexual abuse, draws a distinction between tragedy and malice:

> In the case of tragedy, he or she causes evil despite his or her good intentions or efforts. With malice, the causation of evil is the explicit purpose. The postulated actor's intention is what distinguishes tragedy from malice. *Webster's Dictionary*, for example, defines malice as the intent to commit an unlawful act or to cause harm without legal justification or excuse. Sometimes the term is used in an even more restrictive way as referring to a deep-seated, often inexplicable desire to see another suffer. This, one could say, is real evil. From this

perspective, malice is the ethical identification of the other person as responsible for evil deeds.[6]

This may be a useful distinction when we look at causes. Some people are victims of natural circumstances, of being in the wrong place at the wrong time. Other people are victims of deliberate acts of targeted violence in which they are systematically used for the purposes of another's gratification. Some people – I believe this is true for Jesus – are victims of the violence of the world because they choose to make a stand against the destructive forces of their day and choose to live in a way that is so radical they will almost certainly be killed. But they live with the possibility that through their actions it is possible that there will be such a radical change of heart that violence will be rejected and they will be free. Others do not have that hope of suffering for any constructive outcome at all.

This distinction between tragedy and malice may be useful in understanding where responsibility lies and what an appropriate pastoral response would be; it is still, I think, a reflection that seeks to understand the perpetrator rather than the victim. Surely, for all victims, including Jesus, destructive violence is always tragedy.

So, let us go back to our question about forgiving and forgetting. How are we coming to understand forgiveness from the point of view of someone who has been abused? We return to Jesus, to the act of crucifixion which we now understand is a malicious act, because it is an act of violence against a man of peace. Jesus may have turned temples, challenged the authorities and spoken words of contradiction to the authorities, but to crucify him was an unacceptable violation of power. The death of Christ is the result of a deliberate act of destruction by people in power to a person who has committed no crime. The result is not simply to endeavour to pick up the pieces and begin again, but rather to critique the whole of life from this point. The question-mark of the cross is one that challenges every act of destructive power, and asks the world, 'Does it have to be like this?', and brings the story of humanity into a different light. Those who bore witness to the events of the crucifixion also bore its pain: not least Mary, whose labour of love brought her, like so many mothers, to personally confront the tragedy and malice of the world.

## Transformed hope

In the face of this malice, Jesus says to those who followed and bore witness, who mourned and wailed for him,

> Daughters of Jerusalem, do not weep for me, weep for your-selves and for your children. For the time will come when you will say, 'Blessed are the barren women, the wombs that never bore and the breasts that never nursed!' Then they will say to the mountains, 'Fall on us!' and to the hills 'Cover us!' For if men do these things when the tree is green, what will happen when it is dry? (Luke 23.28–31)

Here is a person in despair, isolated, violated and at his end. This is the same person who both told his disciples to forgive 'seventy times seven times' and yet to 'brush the dust from your feet' and yet here hangs within these many contradictions. Moments after his cry of outrage in which he says it would be best for women to be barren, he gives up his life saying, 'Father, forgive them, for they do not know what they are doing', and to the unrepentant criminal dying beside him, 'Today you will be with me in paradise.'

Why does Jesus die? How does this dying person embody hope that the world can be transformed, hope that there could be another way for people to live together in respect both for each other and God? Whatever this hope signifies, he chooses to die for it, to put his body where his belief hangs. And Jesus is surely defeated. The cross of Christ appears to signify nothing but the victory of the abuser over the abused, the powerful over the vulnerable, the short-term over the eternal.

And yet, within all this maybe we have been asking the wrong question; we have been asking the question from a position of power rather than from the perspective of '*sur vivre*'. The question-mark of the cross asks not, 'Why did Jesus die?' but rather, 'For whom did Jesus live?' We find the question in Luke 24 as the women search the empty tomb and the angels ask, 'Why do you look for the living among the dead?' And as we allow the death of Jesus to ask this question, we realize that we are not yet at the end of this story but at the pivot. We are at the threshold of a new way of understanding life; the door is opening, not closing. This transformation can only happen if we begin to see Jesus from the point of view of one who seeks to '*sur vivre*'. He is not a man who has had everything and relinquished it for a greater good, he is instead a man who has been lost in the Temple and discovered his identity through living in another way. Jesus is not lost on the cross, Jesus is found. He and those around him see what he has become. He embodies the God to whom he is related. The cross of Jesus is not simply an event but a way.

'So,' I hear you ask, 'what about justice, what about restitution and reconciliation?' I want to respond, 'Not yet.' For now, we need to stay with Jesus on the cross because it is here we begin to glimpse the paradoxical truth. At this point of total desolation the power of the perpetrator is being torn from top to bottom. It is this breaking of the bonds, the defiance of death through the authentic strength of victimized humanity that begins to show another way. Jesus does not replace one power with another, but turns vulnerability into strength. He is not defeated, he is never less than himself, but in his dying he claims a new relationship with those he loves and to the earth of which he is a part. The reason that we know this is because it is recognized by two dying thieves, one of whom names him 'Christ' and the other who declares him 'innocent'.

We know it also because of a group of people at a Khulumani hearing, who bear the scars of many terrors, who can sing with the heartbeat of their African rhythms, 'God of opportunity, use me.' The song is the song of '*sur vivre*' – a reworking of Julian's assertion, 'You shall not be overcome.' This is the sign of a different way, a way of resilience in the face of victimization, and life in the face of death; the way of '*sur vivre*' begins to tell a different story. Jesus is not so much victim as an embodiment of another way of living. And forgiveness comes from discovering the inner strength and solidarity to claim this and go on living into the future.

But a word of caution; in case we are in danger of turning crucifixion, domestic violence and sexual violation into a concept, some kind of noble act to sanctify suffering, let us remind ourselves again that they are a traumatic aberration of human behavour. The cross is a symbol of torture and death, it signifies our inhumanity to each other, the destructive forces of violence. This violence is not a good thing, and yet through the cross we are shown a different way, not just an ethereal spiritual message but a practical, earthed response to the forces of violence that conspire to overwhelm us. So for a moment maybe we should pause and think of these practical steps implied by the way of Jesus. What is this 'way', how do we recognize it, and what does it mean in practice for ordinary, troubled humanity? I want to suggest four hallmarks of the way of Jesus. It is, I believe, real, relational, questioning and optional.

## A real way

First, the way of Jesus is a real way. That is, Jesus calls us into the naming of things. Abuse is real and we are not called to beat about the bush but to name those things that diminish the possibilities of being fully alive. That does not mean that we are surrounded by abuse at every turn, but breaking free from cycles of violence means recognizing them for what they are. Abuses need to come to light, to be recognized as real possibilities within all societies. As one person who spoke of abuse said to me, 'Barbara, you are going to have to believe the unbelievable.' We have to open our ears to the stories that are being held silently around us, and to our own story. Peter, the one who denied that he even knew Jesus, was the one who failed to recognize what was happening around him. The one who denies loses sight of the pivotal point of the cross. In order to break the cycles of abuse around us, we must first recognize and name them. People who have experienced abuse do not have two heads and wear a label; in every company of human beings there will be those who '*sous vivre*' – living underneath a story of abuse, silent and alone. We need to be people who both acknowledge this to be a fact and, however painful, be honest witnesses, standing alongside and among those whose stories are coming to birth, in turn bringing our own stories to birth. The way of Jesus is not fictional wishful thinking but real, earthed, honest and incarnate. We must learn to listen to the experiences of others and our own experiences, however difficult, confusing and nuanced they are. We must trust that however dark these places of abuse, they are not devoid of God's grace and love. However terrible or traumatizing, we need to find the strength within to recognize and name abuses, to be honest witnesses to the story-telling and to give voice to the pain.

## A relational way

The way of Jesus is relational. Outside Chester Cathedral there is a sculpture of the Trinity. It is a wonderful piece of work in which three figures intertwine with both tenderness and strength. One figure stands centrally, upright and somehow detached; another stands with arms outstretched to shield, and the third weaves between, stooping down with an open hand to protect the feet of the central figure. Walking around this fine piece of work, we can begin to sense that we are part of this interaction, resolved and vulnerable, strong and dependent. It speaks strongly of the relational nature of God. I believe the way of Jesus is relational because God is by nature relational. The pain of abuse is pain within God. Standing together as disciples around the foot of the cross is probably the hardest thing we are ever called to do as human beings. Yet, the way of Jesus is a way of friendship and solidarity. We are allowed to get things wrong, to be confused or afraid, to misunderstand or to say the wrong thing; but the important thing is that we keep returning to be alongside those who sense they are lost, remaining in solidarity with others and with ourselves, finding strength within powerlessness.

## A questioning way

The way of Jesus is a questioning way. The powerlessness of abuse sometimes leads to us feeling lost, not knowing the answers, bewildered or out of our depth. Just as Jesus was found as a young man lost among his questions, so the way of the gospel is a questioning way. We are not required to live out of certainties, but out of grace. This means that we have to discover a way of being that is not afraid to know the truth. What has threatened the survival of the earth most in the last centuries is possibly the aggression of those with religious or cultural certainties. The cross does not symbolize certainty but the embodied permission to live under faith's question-mark, the question-mark of life and death, of love and destruction, of betrayal and friendship. There is a deep strength that lives authentically within these questions.

Why are we called to live our questions? Because of the God who is listening to us, the eternally attentive Creator who listens to the earth and her people. God bears witness to the struggles, to the silences and to the anguish, and it is this listening that is the fuel for justice-making and peace. Being attentive is not a passive activity but rather it is a mission statement for transformation, because if we really listen to the earth and to each other we will be full of longing and passion for justice. This passion will be the inspiration to live in ways that allow people to be both autonomous and related. Justice comes when difference is not only honoured, but seen as the creative possibility for 'sur vivre', for resurrection. Within this process, living with and within diversity is perhaps our biggest challenge because it brings us to question our own assumptions and prejudice. Living as boundaried individuals, we both claim the space to be ourselves and honour the different needs of others to inhabit safe enough spaces and creative relationships and to flourish.

## An optional way

Finally, I believe this way of Jesus always has to be an optional way. It cannot be a coercive way. There should never be pressure to conform to it because a religion without choices is a sect and too easily has the danger of becoming an opportunity for further abuse. Thank God for Thomas who was courageous enough to doubt because it is he who has given us all permission to live with healthy scepticism. The way of Jesus is an optional way, it is about life and hope in the face of despair and death, but life and hope are gifts, not demands. If religion brings destruction or diminishes life then it should be banished from the earth because it will simply destroy us rather than give us the way to '*sur vivre*'.

The forgiveness, the 'for-giveness' of the cross, is not a vocation of pretence but a real and earthed call into the relational, attentive way of Jesus. It calls people from the isolation of the edge to the realization that this edge is in fact a threshold. And here we are back with mission, the free offering of a way of life that is both transformative and incarnate. The way of Jesus offers the choice of another possibility of becoming, a threshold to life as opposed to an edge of destructive evil.

> . . . 'taking up the cross' in costly discipleship means a willingness to struggle against evil, for the sake of fullness of life, for the 'bringing back of beauty'. It does not mean the passive acceptance of imposed suffering. Rather it means resistance to any pain or violence unjustly inflicted and an affirmation of abundant life for all. It means prioritizing love and justice inseparably intertwined.[7]

Love and justice, inseparably intertwined, is the stuff of life and story. Let me return to my friend Alison, whose jump from a bridge found me, as described in Chapter 1, sitting in a car park outside St James's Hospital in Leeds wondering how to face her tentative hold on life. Alison and I met when we were both Methodist wives of

Anglican students in a theological college. Our respective bishops had been pursuing us to be 're-confirmed' so that our husbands could continue in training. We became friends in our resistance to the coercion. After the vicissitudes of theological college, our paths diverged, me to Liverpool and Alison back to her native Yorkshire and the hardships of rigorous industrial action during the miners' strike. Alison's father had been a miner in the West Yorkshire pits, her mother had struggled to raise a growing family who took it in turns to have the shoes to enable them to go to school. Alison's childhood was one of desperate poverty, struggle and determination to survive. After leaving college, her return to the area and to the political ramifications of a strike that was a community act of resistance to the pit closures caused Alison deep inner struggle. Families were literally penniless. During this time also, Alison's family discovered a heart weakness in its male line – probably due to the ongoing hardship, stress and poor diet Alison's brothers began to die, along with her mother who had become worn out in the struggle and grief. After her mother's death she was prescribed anti-depressants by the local GP and was finally admitted to hospital with serious depression. In the hospital she was given drugs to which (it was later discovered) she had an allergic reaction. Rather than relieve the depression, they exacerbated the symptoms. The doctor who had prescribed the medication knew little English, the care team failed to notice that Alison had wandered from the hospital ward, and that is when she jumped from the bridge.

Alison had been brought up in the local Methodist chapel; church and culture were integral parts of her identity. The desire of the bishop to 're-confirm' her was not simply a matter of church protocol but rather an assault on identity. She did manage to resist his offer to 'lay hands on her' one afternoon when he called round to the house for a cup of tea. With much of her foundational story shaken – her Methodist roots and her identity within a mining community – she was soon engulfed in a depression. She said to me from her hospital bed, in agony from a crushed spine and heels, 'I didn't want to die, Barbara, I just didn't know how to go on living.'

What is forgiveness? Well, to follow the logic of this chapter, Alison was subject to both tragedy and malice. Some of her circumstances were brought about by events beyond her control, others were deliberate acts to undermine her sense of identity. Her journey to '*sur vivre*' began when she found the courage within to name what had happened. This has meant a court case in which the health authority apologized for gross incompetence, and in which a physician was flown back from India to give evidence but seemingly had insufficient English to understand what the barristers were asking him. This 'naming' has been a hugely painful process, both physically and emotionally. Despite countless operations to rebuild her spine and feet, Alison was not expected to walk again but is now out of a wheelchair for significant periods each day. She has had to mine a deep seam of personal resilience, in which she has come to believe that her life is both significant and possible, and she has found a new web of significance in commitment to regeneration of the mining community in which she still lives. In fact, as I write this, Alison is preparing for a visit to the Secretary of State to discuss town centre regeneration, the building of a museum and heritage centre, and has just completed her MA in heritage studies. She believes that the young people of the town should understand their history and be encouraged to be proud of their area and themselves. In Alison's story we find the process of forgiveness lived out of ongoing bodily pain. She is committed to speak of her experience, but not to be stuck within it. Her inner fortitude brings her to a powerful commitment to justice and opportunity in her community. Forgiveness is to break the bonds of obligation that have undermined Alison, to remember the past differently and in her new-found ability to live life into the future. Alongside the Khulumani women she could sing, 'God of opportunities, use me', although, being the good Methodist that she is, she is more likely to launch into 'Love Divine, All Loves Excelling'!

Forgiveness is a future activity, built on justice, resilience and the desire to live life differently. It is a process of picking up the pieces and forming them into something else. It also involves a certain bloody-mindedness which asserts that our lives are worth living despite all the odds. Alison and I are still Methodists, despite the bishops' best attempts to make us conform! And while we will always struggle to be comfortable within church communities, and while Alison's body will always carry the pain and scars of 'not knowing how to live', there is a sense that we have broken the bonds, have prevailed and are being transformed. On a good day, we are able to see that we are becoming something different, which becomes more exciting than terrifying – and, within it all, we will always be friends.

'Do you remember seeing Katy in her wedding dress?' I ask my mother as we cast about for conversation one wet Saturday afternoon. She looks puzzled, then a smile lights up her face, 'Yes, yes I do!' she says, and while I doubt she could answer any question at all relating to the details of the event, somewhere deep down in her frail body, I have no doubt that she does remember – somewhere in her bones.

# Chapter 6

# Redeeming Relationships

After the trial and death of their friend, the two companions decided to walk home. There was little point hanging around and there was a lot to talk about. Not much of the events of the past few days made sense – they had hoped for so much and now it had all turned to dust. The violence and destruction seemed senseless, and they longed to leave it all behind.

If there is one thing that identifies the disciples after the death of Jesus, it is that they were confused and afraid. This is, of course, a direct consequence of any trauma, let alone one in which so much divine hope was invested. We find women terrified in a garden, men huddled behind locked doors and disgruntled fishermen engaged in displacement activity. Abuse and grief are very closely linked. Grief, as we know, takes many forms but is characterized by a number of stages – disbelief, denial, loss, guilt, anger, sorrow, all come before any kind of integration. But this is not necessarily a linear process with one emotion following neatly behind another. Grief takes its own path and will come to the surface or be held in check according to its own emotional journey. As we discussed in Chapter 2, people who have suffered abuse often feel unsafe in their bodies. Their emotions and thoughts may feel out of control. They can also feel unsafe in relation to other people. To secure sufficient safety to begin to unbind the experience of abuse it is necessary to acknowledge its trauma and its effects, to grieve and endeavour to restore a sense of control over the body and the environment the body inhabits. It is also necessary to form appropriate relationships and to establish communities that are both honest and integrating.

Luke's Gospel is all about people and things being lost and others waiting or searching. It tells of the coin, the sheep, the Samaritan, the Prodigal Son that were all lost, as was Jesus himself, left behind in the Temple. A person who has experienced childhood abuse may well sense that part of them has been left behind. They can lose the ability to integrate childhood experiences into adult life. In extreme cases this 'left behind' child splits off from the rest and is expressed as a separate personality, maybe of a different age or gender, and can gain control of a victim's life. There is an ongoing sense of powerlessness, betrayal and stigmatization. The child's body has been invaded and part of the adult's personality may be stuck in angry expressions of invasion and immaturity. This can also be true of societies, institutions and nations as well as individuals. Israel was an invaded state and those who grieved for Jesus had hoped for liberation, not simply for themselves but also for their people. The grief they express is greater than their own disappointment: it is the loss of hope for everyone. We hear this expressed in the words of the grief-stricken disciples on the road to Emmaus, 'We had hoped that he was the one to redeem Israel.' It was as if all their hope had been left behind in Jerusalem with the death of Jesus.

If we have lost, then we experience grief for that which has been lost, both for ourselves as individuals and also for ourselves as communities and nations. We hear this expression of loss in the lament of the two on the road to Emmaus: 'We had hoped . . .' (Luke 24.21) but we also hear it closer to home. In England we too live with a legacy of grief. The British lived through the trauma of the Second World War without consciously voicing national grievance or regret. It is as if part of our story was left behind, not integrated into our national identity. After all, we were supposed to be the 'winners' and needed to get on with the job of reconstruction. There is not one member of my mother's generation who did not suffer loss of some kind, but it is couched in the language of victory and glory. No wonder that as a nation we lack confidence in our own identity.

It is not surprising that we harbour national grievances, because we have never really expressed national grief. It is as if we have left the certainties that were supposed to come with victory and remain shaking our heads saying, 'We had hoped.' This is why '*sur vivre*' is not simply for individuals who consider themselves survivors, it is a way that can begin to allow such stories to emerge and bring a different way of being for communities and nations. Like the disciples on the road to Emmaus, we need opportunities to be real about grief and let it take its course. They are some of the saddest words in the Bible, 'We had hoped . . .' and this loss of hope can also be heard in the grievances expressed between people today. Grief is endemic – sometimes voiced, sometimes bubbling to the surface at unexpected moments and sometimes being expressed silently in depression or despair or bursting out in civil disobedience, grievances or violence. Communities can often feel left behind, abandoned – a lost cause.

At the moment I live in Liverpool, a city with roots in exodus people who fled their homes because of the Irish potato famine and which is often accused of having a victim mentality. If individuals deal with loss by experiencing grief, then cities and nations often express similar emotions as grievances. While Liverpool's history has elements of loss and destitution, the most recent grievances concern the repercussions of the murders of James Bulger, Anthony Walker and Rhys Jones, the disaster in the Hillsborough football stadium and the imprisonment of Michael Shields – a football supporter imprisoned for alleged assault after a match. The city still has posters that say 'Justice for James' or 'Hillsborough', 'We will never forget' or 'Michael come home'. And if you think this is an aberration of Liverpool behaviour, at least this city has the confidence to express its grief. Seemingly London carried on regardless after the bombings, but there is tangible nervousness around fire sirens, and I would challenge a Londoner to name murdered teenagers in the way that Liverpudlians can. South Africa looks forward to a new era but the numbers of armed police and the sale of security gates soar. And there are curious silences in South America despite the challenges from human rights campaigners and the mothers and grandmothers of the disappeared.

Grief is endemic in our society, not only because we have lived through war and trauma as a nation or in our local communities but because we are also home to groups of people who collectively face the after-effects of trauma or abuse from around the world. Mike Stein, in his work on resilience with young people,[1] reminds us that young people in British society represent a population that is always on the move. In 2002, along with the 8,000 British young people who moved in and out of care, there were over 6,000 unaccompanied asylum-seeking and refugee children and young people supported by local authorities. These children will have experienced rejection, abuse, disruption and loss of significant adults. They may have been recruited into military service, been compulsorarily re-educated or been prohibited from practising cultural or religious beliefs.

Transient populations move in and out of cities and countries, bearing with them collective as well as individual grief. Their loss is not simply of an individual kind but collective and multiple. Stein highlights the paramount importance of stability to fortify young people's resilience and enhance their chances of survival. He describes these stable points as 'redeeming relationships'. These redeeming relationships are not simply the work of carers or professional support staff. Stein tracks the progress of these young people from 'victim' to 'moving on' and sees a clear trajectory whereby they are, with time and attention, able to integrate their experiences and gain confidence and life skills. Redemptive relationships are key to engagement with this process as they enable the young people to find stability and a network of support and mutual trust.

This need to form creative and redeeming relationships is essential not just for individuals but for the survival of societies, for all nations rather than simply those which are recovering from a devastating history. The call to make places of stability in which there is safe enough space for stories to be told, appropriate boundaries negotiated, diversity honoured and creative relationships formed, is not simply so that damaged people can have a chance to flourish but so that the whole of life can become different. In short, I believe that if we can really listen to those who '*sur vivre*', we will be given a clue as to how to transform our society and our earth so that we can all live in a different way. As the grieving friends said on their walk to Emmaus, 'We had hoped that he was the one to redeem Israel.' The loss expressed by those who '*sur vivre*' is for the whole nation, not just for themselves. And, as on the road to Emmaus, the one who accompanies them on this journey transforms not only individuals but shows us the way to transform all human relationships and our relationship with the earth.

## Redeeming communities

So, the transformation brought about by such redemptive relationships is a collective call to all of us to live in a different way. We have discussed how our chances of '*sur vivre*' are enhanced if we live within relative rather than absolute safety and acknowledge the importance of the webs of meaning that we are able to weave for ourselves. We have also referred to subversive rather than heroic texts, the need to be heard from beneath a dominant success narrative and to have sufficient space to find power to make life-giving choices. The psychologist Judith Herman describes a three-stage model of recovery adapted for use in diverse situations where complex trauma has become chronic and debilitating.[2] The three stages are, first, establishing safety; second, remembering and mourning; and third, reconnection and the reclaiming of identity. What implications does this three-stage model have on us as collections of individuals, as communities, societies and nations? What practical steps can we take as a society to discover redemptive relationships and communities? How could we find safe enough space for grievance to give way to grief? How would it be possible to enable people to rediscover those parts of childhood that have been misplaced or lost? And how could we encourage stability and continuity in the face of a modern push to progress, quantitative results and a postmodern desire for relativism?

First, let us consider Herman's imperative for establishing safety, not just for individuals but for communities. We have already discussed the need for us as individuals to take appropriate risks and live in 'safe enough' spaces rather than wrapped away from every danger. But, if our true life depends on establishing sufficient safety for all to flourish, then there needs to be a collective incentive to negotiate a way of living together. '*Sur vivre*' is not an individual activity: it is a collective resolve, a covenant whereby power is redistributed for mutual benefit and growth.

There is a hymn in the Methodist hymn book which begins, 'Lord, thy Church on earth is seeking thy renewal from above, teach us all the art of speaking with the accent of thy love . . .'[3] I have always liked the concept of the 'accent of God's love'. It implies that our way of being can be marinated in grace, that we can begin to skew our lives and our society in a particular way, and, like lines on a railway track, a small realignment at a set of points can lead to a change of destination down the line. So what is the accent of God's love in the face of a society that is prone to grievance because of unresolved grief?

On the road to Emmaus, within the conversation with a stranger, the two disconsolate disciples began to hear the accent of love alongside them. But first the stranger heard them give voice to their gut-wrenching lament, 'We had hoped.' This lament is the beginning of the grieving process, the expression of total abandonment and loss. This is true for individuals and for communities. A bereaved person may wail at a graveside, an abused person may mourn the loss of love, of stability, of parenting, of innocence, of childhood; and a community can lament its loss of purpose, vision, protection or trust. We may choose to paper over these times of lament, they are uncomfortable, raw and honest, but unless they are experienced we will not grieve. There needs to be a naming of loss, the awful starkness of it, the emptiness and desolation. As communities and nations we need to express, 'We had hoped . . .' and begin the mourning for our disappointments, our lack of integrity and the things that have gone horribly wrong.

There has been a conversation at our local survivor support network as to whether to use the word 'shit' in the publicity material. Among other things, the support worker wanted to put on the leaflet, 'Abuse is shit'. A lengthy discussion has apparently ensued as to whether the use of the 's' word might be counter-productive to winning the hearts of the kind of people who might support the work. But, whatever our views about using this language in publicity leaflets, it does get to the point. Abuse is surely crap, and this is an honest way of naming it as just that. Living with the accent of God's love is not to retreat into a haze of polite and mythical perfection. People don't suffer in the abstract, they suffer in their bodies and minds. Feelings of rejection, abandonment and powerlessness are rooted in concrete events, places and times. Not naming the reality of abuses, pretending that it is somehow in the private realm, is to collude with the perpetrators. It forces people into cycles of silence. It is also a way of increasing fear of abuses so that they become disproportionate. Most people do not abuse, most people are not abused. Speaking in the accent of God's love is to endeavour to form creative human relationships that resist the idea of a perfect world and begin to name human experiences for what they are. As the Khulumani counsellors knew, speaking with the accent of God's love gives the possibility of opening up spaces for honest conversation, a safe enough space to 'say it how it is'. This is a call not just to our words but to our demeanour, as individuals and within natural and built environments. It means that as individuals we are required to open up spaces of frank conversation and to nurture encounters where such exchanges are possible.

This intentional reconstruction of healthy communities is essential for us to '*sur vivre*' within an urban environment. If we are able to promote an air of honesty, with safe enough spaces built into the bricks and mortar of our homes and cities, then we are beginning to speak with the accent of God's love. What does this mean in practice? It means that Liverpool, and indeed all cities, needs to honour and actively sustain radical places of encounter such as independent bookshops, places where ordinary people can afford to drink coffee at a reasonable price, have opportunities for conversation, and places of recreation and restoration. It is not sufficient to construct cities in such a way that they are built solely for commercial or recreational ends without giving space for quiet, playfulness or tenderness. In our joint quest for survival we need to preserve and create places of conversation, where views can be honoured, grievances aired and differences recognized. This is the heart of life for people who have lost heart. As on the road to Emmaus, transformation begins when strangers experience genuine human encounter, when people are able to fall into step with each other and engage in conversations that recognize difference. This is the accent of love in the city: places of true meetings that give room for hope and open-hearted conversation.

So how do we promote such creative conversations and encourage individuals to fend for themselves in neighbourhoods that are prone to fear of the stranger? Mark Davis, in his book *Walking on the Shore*,[4] goes to the root of the word '*conversare*' and encourages the to-and-fro of dialogue that is intended to be an honest and creative exchange of ideas (rather than discussion which stems from the image of two combatants knocking each other to the ground). This, Davis states, is not simply a matter for church groups, but a transformative way of being in any context. The ability to engage with our outer world and converse about it, is a means of bringing heart to our environment as well as to our souls. True conversations work with the nuance and the struggle of a community, they bring things out into the open and name the trauma as well as the delights. Such conversations spring up between friends or strangers who fall into step beside each other with the intention of true listening and the possibility of mutual transformation.

I had just such a conversation as a friend and I walked round Liverpool city centre on the first day of its status as 'Capital of Culture'. We observed the mish-mash of buildings that have emerged over the last few years, and we sensed we could have been anywhere in the world. We saw the huge cranes erecting lift-shafts in yet-to-be-constructed retail and office developments. We marvelled at the new arena that dwarfs the Albert Dock and wondered how this was going to be managed and policed on busy Saturday nights. We walked past the 'Beatles Story' attraction with its canned recording of 'Yellow Submarine' blasting out and wondered where the young men who want to strum a guitar in their suburban homes can find space in which to express their creative energy without complaints from the neighbours. We read a notice that informed us that any group of two or more people was likely to be dispersed by the police. We watched the huge diggers scooping out a channel to join the Leeds and Liverpool Canal to the Mersey basin. And we asked, 'Whose city and whose culture?' We were troubled by the lack of any sense of difference, any possibility that we might be different from other cities in the region, and we expressed our fear of urban unrest when the Scousers see that this has been constructed by financial and soon-to-be-absent powers. Those of us who remain will need to find safe enough space so that those voices that have been excluded can begin to talk from underneath. Liverpool will need encouragement to reclaim its 'strength from within' and to open up honest conversations to enable its residents and communities to survive the scars left by the JCBs. This is not in the cursory activity of consultation during which city councils send round questionnaires in order to bolster the decisions they have already made. It is, rather, a long-term commitment to the organic growth of the city, to the council falling into step beside its citizens. Those who hold power need to see the city as a body which can itself be traumatized and scarred by successive waves of regeneration and in need of places where it can express its pains and dramas. A city longs for redemptive relationships just as much as individuals. It requires honest partnerships between organizations that work for the common good rather than an infrastructure of rivalries predicated on fighting for the same funding. Cities must find their inner strength, their own accents, so that they can acknowledge their history, their journeys and disappointments, rejoice in their vibrancy and break the bonds of past oppressions. If all this seems to have been an opportunity missed during Liverpool's 'Capital of Culture' year which has largely been based on retail and leisure, there are glimmers of encouragement – new music emerging, artistic ventures being expressed, and subversive activity never far from the surface. Time will tell if Liverpool's voice will emerge, will '*sur vivre*', bringing new life beyond grief, blossoming as creative conversation rather than depression or anarchy.

## Remembering and mourning

Somewhere on the road a stranger had fallen into step beside the friends. When he saw them shaking their heads about the things that had been going on, he asked, 'What things?' How could anyone's life be going on normally in the circumstances? But he listened to the story patiently enough – how Jesus had been taken and how the disciples' hopes had been dashed. When they had finished telling the sorry tale, he began to reflect on the bigger picture, letting the pieces fall into place. Somehow in the remembering, some sense of order began to dawn.

On the skyline of Johannesburg there are huge waste sites from gold and diamond workings. As we drove past, I was suddenly conscious that my great-great-grandfather had set sail for this distant country more than 150 years ago to prospect for minerals. In this reconnection with my own story, there was suddenly an acknowledgement that our histories are inextricably linked across the world. Indeed, as we sat as guests in the Khulumani hearing we were painfully aware that our white faces denoted a message of oppression. We not only had responsibility to listen to stories but also to be contrite. Our British accents had to overcome a message of colonialism and discover the accent of God's love in a new way. To engage in such a process is the first step in turning grievance into grief. We are not going to reverse history and make everything all right but rather we are given permission to name the pain and trauma of the past and to begin to mourn all that has been lost, both by individuals and by a nation. In this engagement we must find places of lament, to weep for all that is lost and confess that we are not innocent bystanders. The Khulumani hearing is not a piece of therapy for distant people but rather a process of re-creation, of redemptive friendship for the world. Such redemptive relationships are signs of hope for the '*sur vivre*' of all of us.

According to Judith Herman, the second stage of reclaiming life after trauma is a process of remembrance and mourning. It begins with the reconstruction of the narrative of trauma, retrieving memories and emotions associated with them, transforming them so they are no longer invasive and debilitating. In this way there opens up an opportunity to mourn the loss of the self and the possibilities which were destroyed by abuse. This mourning is not simply a personal matter, but whole communities need to learn to remember and to mourn. One of the greatest losses for British culture is any ability to mourn collectively. We have sanitized death into a package where we are not faced with its embodied reality. Death is about bodies, and to mourn is to miss someone's physical presence, their mannerisms, their smell. In our rituals we hide bodies away, we embalm them, we put them in a box so that we are not faced with the reality of death. Grief becomes a personal matter, something to be 'got over' in a private context, behind closed doors.

This secrecy about death and mourning is not healthy for anyone, least of all survivors of abuse who may experience a vast range of emotions at the deaths of abusers. Colluding with the secrecy of the past or assuming that death turns all hurts and grievances into forgotten history is to reinforce the cycles of violence initiated by perpetrators. People who '*sur vivre*' teach us something very important about death. They remind us that the things that we have forgotten, pushed to the back of our minds, hidden or silenced within ourselves, are still present; that they are part of our identity and if not acknowledged can lead to a pathological disintegration of self or multiple selves. This is true of nations too. If communities suppress their story, forget their past or pretend everything is perfect, they will become pathological or disintegrate. We need to find collective places of lament in which grief can surface before it turns in on itself and becomes expressed as destructive grievances. I was interested to note that one of the artworks planned for the 'Capital of Culture' was a project between a local artist and the homeless guys who sell the *Big Issue*. They were to collect bricks that have been washed up at the edge of the Mersey and build a 'Wailing Wall'. In their gleaning of the bricks, the carrying of them to the garden at the Parish Church, and their construction into a place of reverie, these people, who have often been victims of the dominant narratives of the city, remind us of the collective need for lament, the importance of physical engagement with our suppressed stories.

One of the greatest griefs of Africa is the desolation of the AIDS pandemic. In a society where one in six people is expected to die from AIDS and not one family is unaffected by the virus, there is a sense of corporate lament. Yet, on our visit, we still attended churches where this devastation was described as 'the sickness' and information concerning lifestyle choices or sexual activity was patchy. In the redemptive relationship there is no such avoidance. We must name the terrors that stalk us and steal our future. This is not just the responsibility of Africans but of all of us who live in the context of silences and stigmas. We must find the courage within to speak, to bring our questions out into the open, because the God whose Son died in traumatic circumstances sees and is attentive to all of this and is already grieving. Grieving is not an option, nor is it failure; rather it is at the very heart of God.

We can see unresolved grief turning to grievance very clearly in our British urban context. It is particularly noticeable in the dis-integration of gaps of understanding between generations. I have given up counting how many times the local press refers to 'yobs' or 'hoodies' as though it sums up the activities of the entire younger generation. Discrimination is blatant – the sign at the Albert Dock threatening to break up groups of 'more than two people' does not refer to a couple of middle-aged people wandering around viewing buildings, only to groups of youngsters that might appear to be dis-ruptive. In this, I am not condoning anti-social behaviour, but what

I am aiming to highlight is that we are a society shot through with unresolved grief, and it emerges as discrimination, often against the young. Liverpool is a city that struggles to confess sectarianism, in a country that has never grieved for a war, in a world that has been influenced by its trade in slaves. On the train are young people whose parents were displaced from the slums of the city centre, whose great-grandparents fled for their lives through famine, whose new town communities were built without souls. On the same train are their elders, who believed they had fought a war to provide stability for future generations, who grieve for their loss of health and stability, whose city has lost so many of its landmarks in the most recent round of many regenerations. We need to learn to address our grief and not our grievances; to let go of our anger, listen to each other with respect, acknowledge differences, find the storylines that connect us, and begin to form redemptive relationships. This is the long-term, intentional process – called '*sur vivre*'.

## Reconnection and reclaiming identity

Why, if the disciples were in their right minds, did they invite a man to dinner who was in the process of explaining the whole of the Bible, beginning with Moses? He had already called them fools and interrupted their private reverie. But there was solidarity in this stranger. He reminded them of someone, and offered a redemptive relationship by breaking bread.

Judith Herman cites the third task in recovery as reconnection, reclaiming one's sense of self and place in the world and creating a meaningful future. It is about ensuring protection from further harm, realistic reconciliation with oneself and establishing healthy reconnection with others.

At Holy Rood House it is evident that people who are able to find safe enough space in which to tell their stories, to remember and to mourn for what is lost in the company of therapists, are then able, with time, to move into patterns of healthy reconnection and to reclaim their sense of self and place. After a recent retreat entitled

'Women Breaking Free', one survivor of sexual abuse wrote of her stay, 'We seemed to leave there in a safer place than we arrived, as if held, as if a little more confident about our survival, about where we are and who we are. That is an awesome thing!' Can this awesome thing happen also for neighbourhoods, for nations and communities?

I feel that it is only at this point that we are able to begin to talk about reconciliation. Reconciliation is not simply one individual forgiving another, but rather it is a community's determination to make amends. It is not so much the victim's obligation to forgive, but a collective resolve to restore communities and to live in another way. I believe this is integral to the way of Jesus, not as duty but as gift. Only in this way can we take the guilt away from people who have experienced abuse and collectively put responsibility where it lies. If we could find ways of engagement for our communities and cities and begin to fall into step with each other on the same street, to be trusting when we look into a different face and begin to listen to the stories that bubble beneath the surface of our communities, then that would be an awesome thing!

'Somewhere Else' is a community of people who make bread. I have already mentioned Dave, who used to sell the *Big Issue* on our doorstep and who lived rough in the gardens of the Anglican Cathedral until his recent death. Dave was a survivor if ever there was one, and although much of his history was a mystery to us, we knew that he had had struggles and life was often hard. Dave came to join our bread-making community at lunch times and was known for his jokes and good humour. We all remember and mourn Dave – he is part of our story at 'Somewhere Else'. But much more than this, Dave is part of the story of urban displacement that is everybody's responsibility. There are plenty of people in our city who despise the homeless, who spit on them, kick them or make offensive remarks, as if people choose to live lives of destitution. Homelessness is an inevitable consequence of a society built on assumptions of autonomy, success and the ability of individuals to make rational choices. Homelessness is not just an issue for some who seem not to have made it, but rather a result of how we all live our lives. Home-lessness is everyone's issue, and therefore everyone's responsibility.

I do not want to idolize Dave's life; it was nuanced, complicated, troubled. But Dave taught us a great deal about resilience, trust-worthiness and good humour. And with him we were able to form a relationship of solidarity with others of the street homeless who came to our doorstep. This has implications for the choices we make for our lives, and the imperative for us to challenge the hos-tility of the city towards wanderers. If we really fall into step with people who have experienced abuse or trauma then we will find that the Bible begins to break open a new way, a way of becoming dif-ferent. At 'Somewhere Else' we particularly find this as we remem-ber Dave and break the bread together. We consider the story of the Road to Emmaus to be the foundation story of our community.

When Jesus broke the bread with them, the disciples suddenly realized what was going on. This stranger was Jesus, the one who they thought had been lost! This was amazing, and the others needed to know straight away. Even though it was nightfall they turned on their heels and started heading in the direction of Jerusalem, travelling back along the path they had just taken but which seemed very different now.

Judith Herman believes that a key element of recovery from trauma, where possible, is to 'have a mission'; by this she means meaningful and satisfying work which gives a strong sense of purpose in life. She is not referring to mission in the overtly reli-gious sense. She talks rather of a project, purpose, a future direction to life rather than a continual retrospective. And I don't want to speak of mission in the narrow sense of 'telling people about him who have never heard of Jesus'. Rather, I want to imagine mission as living a way that is so transformative that a whole community will, by its very nature, begin to tell another story. Not by what they say but by how they live. Instead of a downhearted set of defeated people, the disciples begin to tell their story with the accent of God's love. This love has broken into their experience and shown them that they are not alone. They see now that the cross has not been the end of the story but, on the contrary, it is the pivot. From this point onwards they are not without hope. They turn on their heels and head off in a different direction. They are turning from death to life.

But they are not simply turning round in their journey as individuals. This turning-point is the beginning of reconciliation for a whole community, it is the reconnection with the bigger picture, it is the moment when people begin to '*sur vivre*' together, and the hidden, silenced story of victimization and loss turns on its heels to make reconciled, restored and flourishing relationships. There are implications to this turning around, and the process of living out these implications is the beginning of reconciliation.

## Reconciliation?

I am suggesting that reconciliation is the work of all people, not just those who have been abused or victimized. Reconciliation is a process of restoring relationships. It is born out of the experience of loss, of being lost, of mourning and lament that we all experience as individuals, communities or nations, and which victims of abuses suffer most acutely. Reconciliation is not a 'forgive and forget' mentality that is expected to wipe out the past. Rather it stems from opening up safe enough space of truth and honesty and encounters with redeeming relationships – the sort of places and relationships where people who are radically different from each other can fall into step, where human beings can express honestly their loss of hope and begin to integrate their grief and grievances into a creative narrative for change.

Hermanus is a small town on the coast south of Cape Town. Within living memory 'blacks' and 'coloureds' were cleared from these beaches with whips. Nestled between the hilly vineyards there is a community called 'Volmoed', which means 'Full of Hope and Courage'. Volmoed is home to a small yet resilient community of people who have offered a place for hospitality throughout the years of apartheid and who now continue to look for ways of reconciliation. In the chapel at Volmoed is a crucifix made from one of the trees on the farm. It is made of red cedar, and the Jesus it portrays has no arms. It is a striking image of Jesus' desire to embrace the world with his own wounded body. Volmoed is about this sort of courage.

Since the overthrow of apartheid, South Africa has been in a process of transformation, a remarkable journey that has been closely observed by the rest of the world. Throughout this struggle it has depended on strong leaders with integrity from every community. One of these leaders is the theologian and pastor John de Gruchy, who lives with his wife Isobel at Volmoed. John writes of reconciliation:

> Reconciliation is indeed, an action, praxis, movement before it becomes a theory or dogma, something celebrated before it is explained ... reconciliation is properly understood as a process in which we become engaged at the heart of the struggle for justice and peace in the world. That is why any discussion of reconciliation must be historically and contextually centred, a reflection on what is happening on the ground by those engaged in the process.[5]

We witnessed this engagement with 'what is happening on the ground' when we stayed at Volmoed. We were invited to share a meal with a new group called 'Eisch!' 'Eisch!' is a gathering deliberately drawn together from all racial groups in the Great Hermanus area with the intention of simply getting to know each other and thus working towards greater social cohesion. As we sat and ate and looked into each other's eyes we were witnesses to a growing rapport among the guests. One white woman remarked that she had never sat down to eat with a black person before. Over supper a businessman of mixed race offered to mentor a young black man who was setting up his own radio company. The leader of this new group voiced the rationale behind the group. 'After apartheid fell,' he said, 'we all retreated. We separated into our own communities and this is not enough. "You in your small corner" is not good enough. We need to get to know each other. It's not just going to happen, we're going to have to make it happen.' Such 'getting to know each other' becomes a core of inner strength within communities, a means of discovering the resilience needed to '*sur vivre*'. This is often down to simple human hospitality in which we are able to share food and converse in an environment of mutual respect and companionship. In the city we often have to buy into such hospitality through the facilities provided by restaurants or cafes, but in whatever way we are able to open up safe enough spaces of hospitality, they are places with the potential for transformation and flourishing, as Holy Rood House experiences in its ministry of hospitality and healing and the 'Somewhere Else' community discovers as it bakes bread.

When they thought about it later, the disciples were not sure exactly when the stranger joined them. It seemed as if he had always been there, listening in on the conversation. They were surprised that he didn't seem to know anything about what had been going on, despite the fact that it seemed as if everyone had been involved. They had to share the story from the beginning. It was only when he began to talk about the scriptures that they really began to take any notice of him. It was surprising, then, that they invited a complete stranger back for food. It was something to do with his way of seeing things in a different way, of putting events into context that made them long to hear more . . .

Miroslav Volf[6] talks of this re-engagement with people of difference as the 'Drama of Embrace'. The beginning of this drama, Act One, is enacted when people who are strangers to each other open their arms. This opening of the arms is an indication of having created space in oneself for the other to come – it is an invitation. But embrace is a process, the invitation is open, and Act Two is a waiting to see if the other will respond. Embrace is not an act of invasion but a longing for the to-and-fro of love. Act Three, Volf says, is the closing of the arms in 'a reciprocal act of giving and receiving – the ability to hold, recognize and behold the other (or the self) as an other'. This holding is a place of equal power, where the other is not overwhelmed but recognized and honoured. The final act is the reopening of the arms in an enactment of release, allowing freedom of each to be autonomous, separate and free. What a hugely risky business Volf is describing by the word 'embrace'. How dare he suppose that victims of abuse can ever take such a gamble in the light of everything that has destroyed life for them? Like the Volmoed crucifix, there is a terrible sense of having no arms with which to embrace, a body violated, incomplete, struggling for autonomy rather than risking relationship.

So, where are we left with reconciliation? I return to the assertion that it is not the victim's job to reinstate his or her abuser. The embrace to which Volf refers is a community activity, something we are called to do together. Rather than heaping blame on victims to restore right relations with perpetrators, it becomes the responsibility of all of us to live in such a way that abuse does not happen; and if it does, to cry out in protest, seek justice and bring the stories into the light. Reconciliation is less of a backward attempt to heal the past than an acknowledgement that things have sometimes been terribly wrong and a determination to create safer, more boundaried and accountable places of truth and honesty – as people endeavour to do at Holy Rood House, at Volmoed, in the 'Somewhere Else' community and among the bread makers of Santiago.

These communities are built on a new sort of freedom. They offer places where there is respite from imminent threat, which means there is a sense of mutuality in which it is safe to be oneself without fear of entrapment or physical danger. They are places that enhance confidence in a community's inner strength, where people fall into step alongside each other. They are places that respect and honour difference, that speak with the accent of God's love, seeing diversity as a gift in which to rejoice rather than a problem needing to be solved.

## Hospitality

The name for community embrace is 'hospitality', and here we are back with mission. If hospitality is going to be genuine then it must be honest and open. It must be the kind of embracing hospitality that welcomes strangers in their strangeness and releases them again without pressure or hidden agenda. The 'mission' I speak about is not a subtext of getting people to sign up to church but rather the offering of open, accepting space where there is the possibility of free-flowing conversation and a mutuality of power and respect. And it is not endless hospitality where well-meaning people wear themselves out as countless needy people take unbounded advantage. True hospitality has a covenant engagement, a reciprocity in which a safe enough space is managed for the benefit of all, not just 'recipients'. It is in hospitality that we begin to realize the ordinary nature of embrace. It is in the day-to-day routine of sitting together around the same table, eating ordinary things, engaging in conversation about the things that trouble us, listening to the stories that bubble up from underneath, that transformative, reconciling communities come to birth.

As Mary Grey writes at the conclusion to her book *Sacred Longings*,

> I have suggested that the desiring heart finds true fulfilment in enabling the happiness of others: in hospitality and openness to the other we recover the joyous possibilities of our interconnected selves. We long for authentic experiences of Sacred Presence. We long too for the healing of our broken communities practising relations of intimacy and mutuality.[7]

And here we come back to the dilemma around the word 'intimacy'. What does such intimacy mean for a reconciling community? I suggest we return to Volf's final act in the drama of embrace – the letting go.

Reconciling communities are those which remember that the final act of the drama of embrace is release. They do not hold for long, but encourage the freedom of engagement and disengagement. They are communities that are fluid and yet stable, are both safe and understand their own vulnerability, are peaceful and yet energized. They are places of the Spirit of God, the one who dances among us with a lightness of touch, with gentleness, humour, lament and laughter. Reconciling communities are those that unbind from the dogma of 'ought' and 'should' and long for the flourishing of the human spirit as an expression of individuality, mutuality and freedom. In other words, reconciling communities are those that are real, truthful, gentle and just. They are, in fact, how God is with us as Spirit and Truth.

> And he said, 'You are to be witnesses to it all. I am sending on you the gift promised by my Father; wait here in the city until you are armed with power from above.' (Luke 24.48–49)

Living in the whimsical way of the Spirit is not an excuse for putting the little grey cells into cold storage, or for burying the head in utopian sand. The Spirit is neither an idiot nor a wimp. In order to unbind the power of abuse, the Spirit will have to enter some dark places, crack open destructive relationships and challenge oppressive systems. This is not the work of some ethereal unseen body but the intentional activity of gritty, determined and resilient communities: communities that will risk being overcome in order to bring about change of heart and may well be characterized by determined waiting rather than instant results, as the disciples waited in Jerusalem hoping for the power of the Spirit.

But waiting is not a passive act: it is an act of solidarity. Communities of reconciliation are called into such solidarity with victims. Indeed, they are often victims themselves. Within all this chance and fragility they are called to be places of stability. This is the work of the Spirit – to hold on, despite all, so that no one is lost. The hope of such communities is that they are held within the bigger story of a Christ who is returning; not as a forlorn hope when all has failed, but in the body of people who come with wounded hands and sides.

In another age, St Benedict wrote of this need for stability, and saw this as the key to a community's sense of cohesion and obedience. While we may want to phrase this differently for our postmodern world, it is clear that 'holding fast to that which is good' is an important motif for those driven by progress, possessions and desire. (And it also provokes a conversation concerning the Methodist commitment to itinerancy!) A stable community is one in which reconciliation is possible because there is a covenant commitment to relationships. Stability doesn't mean stasis. It is not permission to hunker down into the same old rut. Rather, it expresses a desire to go deeper, persevere in relationships and to fall into step with those who are encountered in the process. Reconciling communities are those which open up intentional places for listening, grieving, learning, repenting and beginning again. They are places of lament rather than grievance, 'turning round places' which give sufficient time and attention to be with those who are radically different, and open-hearted places of hospitality and enlivening conversation.

Here we find ourselves once again holding a mirror to the beginning of the story, to Simeon and Anna in the Temple, who waited all those years for their time to come – a time when a stranger was placed into the embrace of their old arms and as they, like the two on the road to Emmaus, began to see their nation's history coming to birth in a new way. And now the shadows of Simeon and Anna are joined in their waiting by the disciples who also stay in the Temple, waiting and wondering what would happen next in this extraordinary story of a divine, redemptive relationship. And others join in this waiting and wondering too, the bread makers at 'Somewhere Else', the Khulumani community in their listening hut, the people of Liverpool in their vibrant city, those who hold fast at Volmoed, the women who bang their pots, the attentive counsellors at Holy Rood House, and people the world over who begin to name their abuses, previously kept silently behind closed doors. This solidarity in loss and grief and waiting is the stuff of the Gospels. And so it is too for a couple of friends who have been trampling down the paths in Laura's allotment as we cradle hot coffee in the embrace of our gardening gloves and wait for the first signs of spring.

# Chapter 7

## Surviving Church

The listening God, becoming among the lost in the life and death of Jesus, Spirit-dancing among the strangers and the vulnerable of the earth, is also the God of the Church. In a conversation with Theophilus, Luke moves his story into the Acts of the Apostles where a traumatized group of disheartened followers becomes transformed into articulate witnesses to a divine and redemptive relationship. They are led by the Spirit into a new way of life. They emerge from under an experience of victimization and trauma to become radical followers of Christ. The resurrection not only re-fashions their national understanding but also motivates a community of sharing and hospitality.

And yet the Church in twenty-first-century Britain is often known for its lack of motivation, inability to listen and a drastic decline in attendance. The demise of the Church has been well documented. It is often a dismal reflection on a faith community's inability to engage with culture, to be attentive to personal story and to witness to a radically different and transformative lifestyle. In the Methodist 'Time to Talk of God' report[1] we read of the tendency to identify taking on a church role as synonymous with discipleship and the failure of many congregations to acknowledge and work with diversity. The Church is often characterized by being narrow minded and a place that is not conducive to honest conversations about life and faith. How then can the Church 'sur vivre', and how can ordinary people witness to the story of God that bubbles up from underneath the dominant narratives of individualism and acquisitiveness that dominate our neighbourhoods? What will enable vulnerable people to be included within faith communities in a way that will lead to the flourishing of all?

If I think back through my life, I can trace a frantic succession of schemes and plans to rejuvenate the Church. The 'People Next Door' initiative of the 1960s was an incentive to get my mother's generation to know their neighbours when the realization dawned that post-war modernity had brought isolation and a devastating lack of confidence in pre-war certainties. This was quickly followed by various 'Mission Englands', and now the conversations are all about 'Fresh Expressions' and 'Emerging Churches'. And yet, it appears that all these schemes have made little difference to church growth. The Church is still mostly in decline and is viewed by many, including my own children, as at best irrelevant or at worst danger-ous. So within two generations we have seen the crumbling of assumptions about Church and a sense of loss both numerically and in any consensus about what constitutes the good news. If the Church is going to survive it is not simply a question of re-configuring the existing structures. 'Fresh Expressions' may re-spin the story but they are often simply attempts to re-market rather than radically redefine the Christian community. If we are serious about the future of the Church and individuals flourishing within it, then there is some logic to starting the exploration by conversing with those who have experience of '*sous vivre*'. So, the first mission-ary task of the Church, as it has always been, since Pentecost, is to wait, and listen to those who speak in a different way.

## What Church isn't

Let us remind ourselves that one in six people has some experience of abuse. So, any congregation of seven people or above has the chance of containing at least one person who has experienced trauma of some kind. This is not a call to panic. Churches are not suddenly going to have to act as counsellors, psychotherapists or lawyers. On the contrary, the ordinary congregation is called to be just that – ordinary. People who have experienced abuse need ordinariness, a frame of reference within which to hold memories, a sense of the world being unexciting rather than traumatic. The first job of the congregation, then, is to know what it is not. An ordinary Sunday congregation is not a therapeutic community, it is a gathering of believers, or at least people who are trying to believe. It is a group of ordinary people who are trying to hold their lives in the light of the gospel, a gathering of those who desire to follow Jesus and to discover the work of God in the world. This gathering is endeavouring to discover the motivation of the Holy Spirit to transform relationships between human beings and the earth. The Church is the 'body of Christ', and that is not a perfect body, it is a body that carries the stigmata of trauma on its hands and side. As Christ's body the Church is damaged, vulnerable and scarred. Its calling is not into perfection but into incarnation – being ordinary people, earthed and present in the world, as Jesus was. So, a surviving Church is not necessarily any kind of 'Fresh Expression' (although it might be), but an ordinary group of faithful people who are determined to live in transformative ways. That is, they are going to be ordinary people who want to acknowledge their own vulnerability and explore the diversity that is already around them and within them.

## Power with, rather than power over

How can the Church embody such vulnerability and still be confident about the gospel? Listening to the stories of those who '*sur vivre*' points us to a clue as to how this might be possible. Abuse is about the misuse of power. Power in itself is not wrong, but we need to be aware of who has it and how it is being used. The clue that those who have experienced trauma give us to appropriate use of power is that it should be 'power with' rather than 'power over' that motivates the Church – the power to accompany rather than the power to manipulate or overwhelm. Being a vulnerable community is not a call to 'Anything goes'; rather it is an intentional gathering where power is acknowledged and used to be alongside others. Vulnerability is not about weakness but about strength, the strength to be open to the stories of others without losing one's bearings. In this way the Church is paradoxically called to be both vulnerable and strong – qualities which, we have noted, are the hallmarks of resilience. It is also called to embody redemptive relationships, those that allow enough space for each to be heard and valued. This process of resilience, born both of vulnerability and strength, is a call to a life born of God's grace. So, for the Church to '*sur vivre*' it needs at its heart a willingness to learn ordinary ways to embody this strong, vulnerable grace and in doing so will begin to witness to the God who attends to all people, calls us into the dance of embrace and longs for the flourishing of the earth. There are no short-cuts to such gracious living; we cannot fix the Church quickly with a new scheme that will bring people flocking, but instead we need to embark on a process of realignment and appropriate use of power. It relies on ordinary congregations that speak with the accent of God's love and begin living as communities that embody God's grace. This, I believe, is the beginning of mission.

So, let us return to the themes that we have discovered on our road to understanding '*sur vivre*' and ask how these may apply to a Christian community. In this chapter we will consider what makes safe enough space, how this is denoted in the body language of the Church, how we can become attentive communities, willing to listen to the silences around us, and use this process to enable the Church to both embrace and set people free. And I want to do this by giving some ordinary nuts-and-bolts suggestions alongside some theological reflection. This is not intended to be an exhaustive list but simply designed to provoke a conversation about a different way of thinking, awareness and the desire to become what God's grace intends.

## Waiting

Luke reminds us that the coming of the Church, like the coming of Jesus, began in the waiting times. As Anna and Simeon had waited in the Temple for the advent of the baby, so too the disciples waited for the delivery of the Holy Spirit, wondering and expectant in the annunciation of the promises of God. So often those intent on mission rush into some scheme or plan without first engaging with the silence that comes from this call to attentiveness. Waiting, watching, wondering, is not passivity; in fact, it may be the most productive thing Christians ever do because it is an act of solidarity with the God who attends to us, listens to our every breath, counts the hairs on our heads, and longs for our company. In order to engage with this process of being attentive, to each other and to the earth, there is a need to still our desire for activity and to wait expectantly for the still, small voice of the word of God in our ear. Mark Davis[2] talks of returning to the original charism of our congregations, the gifts that are specifically ours to live. Others refer to the DNA of the Church, the basic units of life that give us our unique identity. This re-engagement with DNA or charism requires a process of waiting within the nothingness and attending to the strange silences of God in our midst. It is within the silence that we will begin to discern what is at our heart.

I consider the year I spent wandering around Liverpool city centre – watching, listening observing the city – one of the most difficult and most productive years of my ministry. Without a gathered congregation to attend to or a building to maintain, I was privileged to be free to take time to listen to the city and to ask what God was up to in the people and buildings of the place. It was also an extremely hard time for me; it would have been much easier to have had a project or pre-determined set of mission objectives. Watching, waiting, listening, attending, call us into a deep level of faithfulness to the God who goes ahead of us. But not all churches have the privilege of no congregation and no building. Mostly we are burdened with the demands of sick parishioners or leaking roofs.

With these constraints, what might be a way of listening to what is at our heart?

We must begin to use our imagination to see how this watching and waiting can be realized in practical terms. It might mean a congregation embarking on retreat, or having a sabbatical from new projects for a year, or worshipping in silence once in a while, or quietly walking the neighbourhood instead of Sunday morning worship, or going into the Mums' and Tots' group to hear what concerns are around – to listen to the community groups that use our premises rather than issue them with edicts. And as we embark on such a process of intentional listening, there is a need to sit down and ask ourselves, 'Where are the silences, where are the silenced? What is it we are not hearing? And who is it that we are not seeing?' This is the starting point of mission, the waiting and wondering, the engagement with absence, the desire to attend to the things and people that are lost. That is not just an incentive to go 'out there' looking for lost sheep, but to connect with the things that we have lost within ourselves – loss of certainties, of the ability to pray, of good relationships between us and our families or neighbours. Silence is the starting point for mission because it not only brings us to a new attentiveness to each other and to the earth but it also cracks open our souls. When Jesus was absent, time and time again he said to the disciples, 'Wait.'

This deep, intentional waiting is the beginning of '*sur vivre*', for communities and individuals alike. Not so that the *status quo* will prevail, but so that alternative, radical voices can be heard. Opening up a sense of silence and waiting within ourselves as individuals and within our faith communities will literally cost us. It might be that buildings have to close in the process or fund-raising activities cease. Although I was on the working party for the 'Time to Talk of God' report, I wish it had been called, 'Time to Listen to God', or better still, 'Time to Know That God is Listening to Us'! It is in this shift of emphasis that we begin to redistribute power for mission in an appropriate way. Rather than those 'inside' the Church aiming to impart their faith knowledge and insights to 'outsiders' in order that they will sign up, we begin to sense a mutuality, a communality in the process of '*sur vivre*'. We are all held within the loving gaze and attentiveness of the same God who listens not only to us as individuals but to the earth which groans in travail. God longs for life, for all life, and for life in abundance. This birthing is God's labour, and the life of all things is dependent on our attentiveness to this process. Such attention offers a mutual power, 'power with' rather than 'power over'. Simeon, Anna and the first disciples knew this as they waited in the Temple praising God. The waiting time was the time of expectancy and anticipation of deliverance.

As, at the beginning of Luke's Gospel, John the Baptist came out of the silence of the wilderness to baptize Jesus, so at the beginning of Acts the disciples came out of their 40 days of waiting to be baptized by the Holy Spirit. Both these baptisms herald the beginning of a new age. In Jesus, John sees the one who is to take Israel to a new relationship with God, at Pentecost this new relationship bursts beyond Israel to a group of strangers. This gathering is equally empowered, each speaking in their own tongue, each expressing the amazement of the new life that has been given to them in ways that all could understand (except the ones who thought they were drunk!). In this story, some talk and others listen; this is the interaction that leads to transformation, to the birth of the first Church.

For this reason our worship also needs times of watching, waiting and listening. And this will not come naturally to all people – it is amazing how many people want to fill up the silences in church with stage whispers! Congregations need to be trained in this process, need to be comfortable with the 'Not yet' of the arrival of the word. Being silent together is a different process from being silent alone. A congregation that is comfortable to share silence has found a place of deep connection and is a missionary congregation.

Silence is as important to liturgy as pauses are in music. It is the balance of silence and song, word and sacrament, activity and passivity that give the heartbeat to worship. Good liturgy holds a mirror to the rhythm of everyday life. But this mirror is not held simply to idealized life, life where no one suffers or is confused or hurt. Liturgy should hold the mirror outwards to all life, and this includes life that has been damaged, traumatized and abused.

## Repent or walk?

If we are to really live our liturgy then we need to hear what it says and what it does not say, how it uses power for some and not for others, how the language of power can sometimes overwhelm and belittle human experience. I want to illustrate this by returning to Acts. A few chapters after the account of Pentecost there are a further two stories side-by-side. In the first of these stories Peter preaches to the crowd and reminds them that they are the ones who have handed Jesus over to be crucified. The reinstated disciple, full of the confidence of the resurrection, makes it quite clear that this group of Jews is implicated in the destruction of the one whom David had foretold would redeem Israel:

> 'Therefore let all Israel be assured of this: God has made this Jesus, whom you crucified, both Lord and Christ.' When the people heard this, they were cut to the heart and said to Peter and the other apostles, 'Brothers, what shall we do?' Peter replied, 'Repent and be baptized, every one of you in the name of Jesus Christ for the forgiveness of your sins.' (Acts 2.36–38)

Let us hold this story in our mind's eye and go on to a second story which follows close behind when we find Peter and John returning to the Temple for prayer (Acts 3.1–10). They discover a man unable to walk, sitting at the Beautiful Gate. Peter looked straight at him, as did John:

> Then Peter said, 'Look at us!' So the man gave them his attention, expecting to get something from them. Then Peter said, 'Silver or gold I do not have, but what I have I give you. In the name of Jesus Christ of Nazareth, walk.' Taking him by the

right hand, he helped him up, and instantly the man's feet became strong. He jumped to his feet and began to walk.

These stories coming so closely together in the text help us to notice two quite distinctive approaches to the two encounters. In the first story there is an accusation; these people have done a terrible thing and need to make a fresh start. In the second story, the man who is unable to walk has done nothing wrong but is suffering from a disability for which he is not responsible. This man needs assurance that things can be different, and through the attention of the disciples he is brought back onto his feet. In the first story the message is, 'Repent!' and in the second story the message is, 'Walk!' The reason the message is different is because the encounter is with different people. The first group is implicated in a destructive act; they have been the ones to crucify Jesus. But the man at the Beautiful Gate is a person who has been victim of something that was not his fault. He is an innocent but lame man, he needs the power and courage to jump to his feet and begin to live. Both messages are still valid. Some need to repent, others need to walk. Traditionally, however, the Church has favoured the message of guilt and restitution over the message of transforming new life. Liturgies are more inclined to use their power to reinstate offenders than help victims back on their feet. This is not to underestimate the world's need for repentance – we are all guilty of sins committed both intentionally and unintentionally – but it is to say that the balance needs to be restored. Time and time again, Luke tells us, when Jesus encounters the lost people of the earth, he calls them to stand on their feet. The gospel is about life.

Perhaps this is most easily exemplified if we consider the language we use in our liturgy, the words that constitute the formal conversations we have in God's company. Usually, worship begins with an encouragement to approach God, who is powerfully above us. We are also exhorted to examine our own souls which will undoubtedly be less than they should be. We have sinned against God through 'ignorance, weakness and our own deliberate fault'.

We come to God as 'offenders' who are called to repentance. This examination of the soul is usually quite brief and does not require us to verbalize a long list of faults. Having searched our heart and expressed remorse, we are assured of God's capacity to reinstate us to right relations. We can be absolved and freed and are swiftly assured of God's pardon. We are assumed to be the ones who have committed faults and are able to confess and start again.

However, these liturgical steps read quite differently for victims who come to church full of guilt and shame, not because of what they have done, but because of what has been done to them. Traditional liturgies call for examination of the heart and repentance, but people who are experiencing abuse do not need to confess their own guilt. Confessing things that have been done *to* us rather than *by* us can lead to further cycles of self-negation. Those who come to church hurting and guilt-ridden do not need this pattern of forgiveness and restitution, but rather require liturgical permission to put blame where blame is due. Their reinstatement comes not by repentance but when they find the ability to claim their lives, and believe they are worth living. If liturgy is able to give them this sense of breaking the bonds that have kept them in submission to those who have inappropriate power over them, then there is given a new hope to 'Live!' They are the people of the second story, needing the command to 'Walk!'

The need to re-visit liturgical language from the point of view of those who live from underneath is not simply an exercise in linguistic niceties, it is a theological imperative. Jesus is the Saviour who was not only lost in the Temple but also turned the tables. He was not content to let power reside where it had always resided, but has lived a life that challenged the dominant narratives of his day and continually called the *status quo* into question. Liturgy is a living expression in our belief in such a Saviour and has an inherent demand to continually question dominant voices and bring the underneath stories to the surface. Our examination of what it means to '*sur vivre*', that is, to come out on top of cycles of abuse and suppression, has brought us to a theological understanding that the scriptures need to read 'from underneath'. This, of course, is not a new idea and has been continually argued by feminist and liberation theologies; however, the transferring of such thinking into church liturgies still has some way to go in the British church. Our liturgies must be helped to reflect such a journey, giving as many doorways into the Church as possible, expressing eternal truths in fresh ways, honouring the stories of the oppressed and silenced. This transformation brings fresh eyes to our way of being as a community of faith. If we are attentive to the process, we will hear different voices speaking to us, which will both challenge and delight.

## Integrating liturgy

Here is a prayer of approach written by someone who has experienced abuse and calls herself a 'freedom fighter' (rather than a 'survivor'). She wanted to integrate all of her experience and begin to claim her life in a different way:

> Encompassing God –
> look what I've brought you:
> strong and vulnerable,
> chaotic and solid,
> still,
> restless;
> the dark, the hidden,
> the as yet unknown.
>
> The laughing, the lightness
> the dance.
>
> A soul
> stubborn in hope
> determined in passion
>
> – the singing space, a breathing place –

> all gathered
> all celebrated
> all holy
> and whole
> in you.

This prayer offers an integrated approach to God, one in which vulnerability and possibility are held in God's loving embrace. The starting point is the human soul's desire to flourish. Its hope is in the integration of resilience and fragility in the company of the holy and incarnate God. It offers a way of approaching God that is deep and nuanced, an acknowledgement that the starting point might be 'Walk!' rather than 'Repent!'.

So, the stories of those who '*sur vivre*' bring us to understand that our traditional and firmly held ways must be heard with new ears. It is not that all that is precious about the tradition will be destroyed or rejected in the process, but rather that if we encourage spaces for alternative voices, liturgy has the possibility of encompassing more people. Worship needs to be paced with silences, with the accent of God's hospitable and transformative grace. It is the song of life, of all life, and must hold within it a desire to crack open its edges to embrace diversity. It needs to give permission to bring the whole of ourselves to God, even the hidden and angry parts and the risk of it all being gathered together again in restored, creative and life-giving ways.

Key to this process is our use of language. It is not wrong to understand God as powerful, but the language of the Church must also reflect how we believe God's power is used. Is God like an all-seeing, manipulative and overwhelming parent? Does God make us do things in which we lose our autonomy or give up our will? Is God's desire always above our desire? It may well be that those who are already powerful need to relinquish their strength in earthly things in order to trust God more, but what of the people who feel that they are powerless? How can liturgy resist the sense that victims are further reduced? Must they find joy in suffering, be patient in adversity or silent in the face of abuse? This appraisal of language is not about political correctness or women's rights, it is a much deeper theological issue.

Language is the currency of expression and as such brings the depth and struggle of human and divine relationship into the light. Language speaks the birth of the imagination, the imaging of self in relation to God. Language is the rich sea from which the deepest longings of the human heart can be drawn. Language is all we have to verbalize our life, it is a gift of the Creator. To be understood is the gift of Pentecost. Liturgical language must not squander these possibilities. It is not simply the means by which we talk about God but is an expression of the deep longing and living of God within us. It helps us imagine who God is for us, and it speaks into the silences and wells up with possibility. What we say and how we say it in our liturgy are of the deepest, eternal significance.

I am not denying that much traditional liturgical language is beautiful, holds resonances of our history, of the biblical narrative that transforms our current understanding with poetry and rhythm. What I believe the path to '*sur vivre*' teaches us, however, is that we need a variety of approaches to God. Maybe I can best illustrate this by considering a key prayer in my Methodist heritage, the 'Covenant Prayer'. In the annual Covenant Service, Methodists say to God, 'I am no longer my own but yours, put me to what you will . . .' This covenant is a truly beautiful expression of relinquishing our selfishness into the hands of a gracious God. It is a prayer by which I claim my identity among the people called Methodists, for whom God's prevenient grace is part of the DNA. But how does this read if we have struggled all our lives to find ourselves worth being loved by God? What if we need help to claim our identity rather than lose it? The words 'put me to what you will' sound very different if we are people who are longing to find our identity in the light of abuse. Whatever the wonders of our heritage, language matters, and our liturgy must reflect our theology, a theology of grace for all people, not just for some. I am not suggesting that we ditch the Covenant Prayer but rather that we acknowledge that for some people it is far harder and less creative than for others. We need to offer alternative approaches to God that offer the prospect of 'walking' as well as 'repenting'.

Liturgy, then, is an expression of faith by the body of the Church, but it is not the monotone one-sided intonation of a boring institution (or shouldn't be!). Liturgy is an interaction between the God who listens and the creation that God attends. It is therefore a relational activity which requires space for full expression of life experiences, held within the eternal story of the divine. In this way, it becomes a conversation, a dialogue, a cerebral and emotional journey, an integration of the senses. Liturgy is the work of the people, a place of puzzling, sorrowing, marvelling and starting again. We squander all this at our peril.

I am reminded of an experience in a small, inner-city church. A new member of the congregation was waiting for the birth of her first grandchild, but after a few months she disappeared. No one liked to make enquiries, but when she returned it was to the sad news that the baby had not lived. Two elderly women in the congregation came alongside her and both in their own way shared with her the loss of their babies, over 50 years earlier. These two old ladies had sat side by side in church all their lives and had never told their stories before. It was only when a newcomer was prepared to be vulnerable among them that they felt able to talk of their sadness and struggle. If two lifelong Christians have held a silence for so long and never expressed the reality of their story, why would we think that new people would feel safe to come to church? A missionary congregation is one in which there is permission to be real, a place where some talk and others listen, where vulnerability and strength are side by side.

Let's take another example. Think of a funeral liturgy that brings comfort to the grieving and assurance of salvation to the repentant. But where is the anger, the lament, the expression of lostness? Where is the place of rage, space in which to express the grief for lost chances, lost childhoods, lost relationships? We cannot assume that death concludes all unfinished business. Funeral liturgies need to open up the cracks of grief, not shovel soft platitudes around them. All this loss is the business of the church community – it is not simply a private matter, a contract between the minister and the bereaved. We should be asking how we can make safe enough spaces for such grieving to happen. Where can people sit to be quiet, to light candles, to express prayers, silently or openly, drop pebbles into wells, be held in the perplexity of it all? The Church of all places needs to be a place in which to be real and to open up safe enough spaces for stories of life and death to surface, because this is the way of Jesus who came for the lost, not the found.

## The body language of the Church

If liturgy is the spoken language of the Church, then there is also the need to consider its body language. By this, I mean the way in which church communities present themselves in unspoken ways. It is said that 96 per cent of all communication is non-verbal, and this is true of institutions as well as individuals. It is these unspoken messages that often say more about mission than the words that come out of our mouths. Let us consider this from the point of view of appropriate boundary setting which we have highlighted as a key factor in '*sur vivre*'. In church communities there are physical boundaries such as doorways, and there are conceptual boundaries such as membership.

First, let us consider the body language of the physical building, in particular entrances and exits. If you are someone who attends church, I wonder whether you have ever stood outside your building and tried to get in? If not, I suggest you set some time aside to take it in turns to walk across the threshold as if for the first time. Then ask yourself whether 'inside' church is a safer place than 'outside' church. The answer to this will depend on a number of things. Is the church aiming to offer sanctuary or community? These are not necessarily the same thing. Is the use of power within church more appropriate than the use of power elsewhere? Does being with Christians imply choices or commands? None of these questions have simple answers, or even single answers. What is needed is awareness in the Christian community of the non-verbal messages that are being signified by physical things such as buildings, fences, noticeboards and thresholds. These are mission questions. There is, for instance, a difference between an intentionally inclusive community and a community that wants to offer sanctuary. Unless there is a clearly negotiated way of interacting, the greater the diversity of people coming to church, the less safe it becomes, Respecting difference is hard work – it is not simply tea and handshakes. Negotiating and maintaining appropriate boundaries is the missionary labour of the Church. Like all mission, it starts with listening to what is longing to be born.

## 'You are welcome at our church!'

What does this mean in practice? Maybe we should take a 'virtual tour' of an imaginary church as if coming at it for the first time. First, let's stand outside and view the church noticeboard. Is the information on it accurate? Does it give not only the time things are starting but also the end point? Does it give a sense of honesty and hospitality or does it say, 'You are welcome at *our* church', meaning that it is ours and you can only be in it if you are going to be 'like us'? Does it indicate where it is possible to find out more, such as a website address, before crossing the threshold? Does the noticeboard give a phone number for the minister that is boundaried, with suggested hours and suggested venue where it is appropriate to make contact rather than open access to his or her home and family? Is there an indication of when informal contact could be made, or a non-threatening opt-out place for conversation before committing to Sunday worship? The church noticeboard is often the first indication of the body language of the church – that is why there are often arguments surrounding it. The best sort of noticeboard is not trying to be clever or indicate a theological certainty but rather gives an honest, open expression of church life, accurate information and the power of choice to the observer.

Now, in your imagination, walk up to the church door. Is it locked? Is it of human proportions? Is it possible to see through to what is on the other side? Who has the keys? Doors signify different things to different people. They can be barriers or thresholds, indicate a place of safety or a place of entrapment. And because people will view them in different ways there need to be a number of options associated with doors. For instance, some people will want to come early to church, arrive unseen and find a quiet place where they can feel safe. Other people will need reassurance, a clear indication of what is going to happen and a chance to off-load. Doors must not be a barrier to entry, and they must not be a barrier to exit either. For the Church to '*sur vivre*' we need to be able to escape church – it should be a community, not a trap!

Having made it across the threshold, there is then the dilemma of where to sit. Some people like company, others space, some need to be near the back so that they are close to an exit, others like to be near the front so they can relate. Clearly, we cannot get it right all the time, but sitting baptismal parties on the front rows might not be the most sensible option, and asking people to move from their selected position can be far too scary. What needs to happen is that the church community presents a series of options, a sense that power lies with the adult who has walked through the door rather than pressure to conform to a set of unknown expectations from the adults who are already inside. Remember, people who have experienced abuse have often been traumatized in childhood and will have bad memories of being overwhelmed or disempowered associated with this time. For the Church to '*sur vivre*' it needs to engage with the mutuality and negotiation of adult–adult relationships rather than child–adult ones. Making people feel like children will make people behave like children. In the case of those who have experienced abuse, there may well be a great deal of defensiveness, or closing down of trust. We know that this is often a pattern in church communities when they fail to behave in adult, honest and boundaried ways.

I could go on for a long time about the way in which church communities deal with conflict – the unhealthy parent–child relationships that can develop between adults when power is not handled appropriately, meetings where nobody actually meets, meals that are governed by committees rather than warm-hearted hospitality, the tick-list for the faith tea! It is these seemingly small matters that lead to the body language of the Church often being pathological, turned in on itself and a place to be avoided.

And if the physical body language is not a large enough dilemma, then there are the conceptual challenges that further the problem. We live in a society that tends to measure success quantitatively rather than qualitatively. Children take SATS, grant-makers measure outcomes, tourist boards monitor day trippers, and politicians count votes. There is a cultural incentive to measure success by numbers. Churches also tend to assess success at mission by the number of bodies that walk across the threshold. There is some kind of logic that says, 'God is in church, therefore people who are in church are with God.' This is to caricature a whole theology that sees those inside church as having God's power, and those outside to be powerless and in need, with the implication that 'church' and 'world' are completely separate entities. But those who seek to '*sur vivre*' remind us that human beings are not able to shed their life experiences by crossing a church threshold. Identity and belonging are closely linked, and the mission of the Church is not simply to engage with the paper exercise of adding members, but to see membership as a possibility for a process of exploration, of discovering what it means to be really human in the light of God's love. Belonging to a church is about discipleship, a pilgrimage of discovery, an opportunity to go deeply into the meaning of experience in the light of faith. Church membership is not only about 'Repent!' but also about 'Walk!'

## A body of bodies that live is a body that lives!

This balance between 'repenting' and 'walking' is not an additional chore for the Church. On the contrary, it signals the possibility for transformation of a mindset that saps energy into a place of flourishing for all. If the Church is a safe enough space for the flourishing of people who have experienced abuse, then all will begin to flourish. A place where people '*sur vivre*' will become a place that survives. A body of bodies that live is a body that lives! A Church that can negotiate safe boundaries, offer attentive and redemptive relationships, help people break free from oppressive bonds and allow stories to surface, is a community of hope. Just as the lame man at the Beautiful Gate went dancing into the Temple in the company of Peter and John, so the Church can be transformed by those who begin to find their own potential. We will break free from being a morose band of guilt-ridden followers trying to support a dying institution and realize that the transformative power of God is closer to hand than we thought. This is not an invitation into shallow emotionalism but rather an opportunity for deep connection, with our lives and with our earth.

In Johannesburg Central Mission, my colleague Chris and I knelt with the bishop behind the Communion table which held bread and wine for the thousands of Zimbabwean migrants who gathered for the weekly Eucharist. In this simple act, we reverenced the mystery of the elements that Jesus has given to re-member the people of the earth. We looked out at a sea of black faces, people who had fled for their lives or who were in search of employment to sustain their families back home who are suffering God knows what. Ordinary people, some undoubtedly rogues, most simply ordinary people just doing their best in desperate times. We knelt alongside the bishop, whose whole life had been taken up with these people and yet was able to include us in the celebration of what God is doing in that place. In the middle of all that struggle and confusion we could sense the integrity of bread and wine, these simple, ordinary things that both bring people together and put people back together. God's intention, made real, that all should live. And we were aware of the integrity of this remarkable bishop who somehow continues to hold this thing together despite the security forces coming later to search for knives and drugs (which they didn't find). It is this sort of integrity, the eucharistic witness of the Church to be both the stigmatized, broken body of Christ, and also the place of sanctuary and new life, that is its hope.

This kind of integrity is not won without cost. All people who have suffered trauma or abuse know the pain of disintegration that comes with their experience, the pain that is carried in their physical and emotional bodies and the dissociation and fragmentation that has been caused. The process of rebuilding trust, finding the language of inclusion and truly attentive places of human encounter, are sacrificial tasks. They are going to cost us a lot more than opening the church door on a Sunday and being friendly to people who we already know. Integrity is a process of putting back together those things that have been dismembered, the slow piecing together of stories, gentle but strong solidarity with the whole of ourselves, not simply the acceptable parts.

In one church where I was a minister, there were long and heated arguments about the position of the Communion rail which had been re-sited during a refurbishment. Rather than a small congregation having to go up steps to a fixed Communion table attached to the back wall of the church, it was now possible for me as minister to move forward and gather in a more intimate space at the front of the choir steps. After a lot of argument, sulking and general disagreement, someone said to me, 'It may very well mean that you feel closer to the congregation, Barbara, but it feels like a fence to me!'

It is only when we begin to be real about these things that we will all begin to flourish. It is not the position of the Communion rail that matters but the manner in which we deal with the disagreement as honest adults under the gaze of the same God – the God who eavesdrops on our conversation. And this manner will be shaped by how we reverence the opportunity for re-membering that the Eucharist offers us. Both as priest and people we need to find ways of honouring the bread, the living symbol of Christ's broken-ness and integrity.

It is such integrity that is the source of holiness, the holiness that is the vocation not only of the Church but also of the earth. Integrity and holiness are not idealized states that will be attained at some future, discernible date, but are a way of becoming that has implications each day. We are going to fail, fall down and have to repent, but we are also going to help each other back to our feet and begin to walk. This is not simply that we have churches that grow, but rather that we begin to understand again what the good news might be. Good news is not about wishful thinking, it is about remembering ordinary messed-up people and the ordinary fragile earth and beginning to attend to our transformation. It is about reverencing the bread. It is Eucharist. It is the calling of the Church.

I went to see my mother yesterday. It was Mothering Sunday, although she didn't have any idea about that. She gets more forget-ful by the day. Her fingers are getting thinner, her engagement ring is loose and her skin is so fragile that it bruises with the slightest knock. Her hands, the same hands that used to grab a dishcloth and wipe the chocolate off my sticky face, have the fragile quality of a bird. She seems to be becoming translucent, as if she is returning to the earth. My relationship with my mother has never been easy: we are too similar and too stubborn to rub along easily. We have fought, sulked, grumbled and chided our way to this point. But I am no longer 17 and she can't remember to be manipulative, so there is a kind of peace evolving between us, an understanding and forgive-ness born out of our struggles and fragility and the connection with a story that is bigger than both of us. We are no longer behaving as individuals who have power over each other, but rather have the strength to be alongside each other. This is a transformative thing.

Like the Church, my mother has seen war and change, loss, con-fusion, new-fangled ideas; but the story that surfaces has a different life when the bonds are broken and transformed. The breaking of the bonds for the Church does not mean a reckless disregard for tradition, wisdom or learning, but rather the gathering of these things together in a different way in the light of a wider under-standing of experience. In particular, this process of transformation can happen when we are prepared to see that our survival is not guaranteed, that we are the crucified as well as the raised body of Christ, and that we must engage with the long-term journey of holiness rather than the short-term seduction of church growth.

This integrated understanding must extend way beyond our church doors; in fact, we might have to relinquish church doors altogether in our commitment to the survival of the environment. Fewer buildings, energy-saving strategies, fair trade, reusable resources, are not just an afterthought following Sunday morning worship. We know that 'Walk!' and 'Repent!' are both critical. Forgiveness lies in the decisions we will make for the future, having listened to the past. Laura and I talk of these things as we sit in her allotment, knowing that the sustainability of such an enterprise is a long-term project. The day-by-day tending of the fragile things that tentatively begin to flourish, the nourishment of the soil for the long term and the desire to work alongside the natural rhythms of the earth and the weather mark this commitment to the future. But there is also a commitment to rout out the destructive forces that suppress healthy growth and to attend to the most vulnerable, both gently and diligently.

*Chapter 8*

# Consider

The challenge in writing this book has been whether or not it is possible to discern what it might mean to survive within different contexts, cultures, experiences and communities. I have sought to express the traumatic and abusive experiences that so many have experienced in an engaged but detached way, and in so doing I have always been in danger of putting my words into the mouths of the silenced with the risk of adding injustice to injury.

And yet, as I have written, travelled, probed and tried to understand, the question 'What does it mean to survive?' has become more crucial. It has become increasingly apparent that our future as individuals and as nations depends on how we address this issue, and so the wrestling, struggle and contradiction that this book represents feel more important as the days go by. I see now that the way in which we attend to each other and to the earth is paramount in our quest to be truly human. Living from underneath the stories of oppression that so dominate the history of God's people and to become the true expression of humanity that our creator longs for is, I believe, both our vocation and our mission.

One of the most humbling experiences of this journey has been the sheer dogged resilience and courage of those whom the world calls 'survivors', the astonishing will to live that is at the heart of the human soul in the light of the most appalling violation and loss. I have witnessed the desire of so many to embrace life, albeit with wounds and scars, and this human determination to begin again and to 'walk' is both astonishing and humbling. I can say that I have seen with my own eyes what Alice Miller refers to in her book: 'For the human soul is virtually indestructible, its ability to rise from the ashes remains as long as the body draws breath.'[1]

During my travels I have listened to survivors of such outrageous abuse that it is a wonder that any human being can transcend it. At Holy Rood House I have heard people speak of multiple rapes, of rituals that have destroyed any fragment of human dignity, of recurring violations of trust, not least within the Church. In Santiago, we visited the camp where the babies of political detainees were tortured in front of their eyes, where adults were kept three to a cell in a space no bigger than a metre square. I saw the remnants of iron rails which weighed down the 'disappeared' as their bodies were tossed from helicopters into the ocean. In South Africa, I listened to the grandmothers who had lost all their children to murdering thugs, who were still fighting for their land, whose bodies bore the scars of atrocities. I have read about Rwanda and Kosovo through the words of Mary Grey and Moroslav Volf, and I have sat appalled at the murderous intentions of humankind, the mass abuses of power and the cruelty and violation of the human spirit that have happened in this world in my lifetime.

There has at times been an overwhelming sense of the silence of God in the face of such violations. Where is the all-seeing, all-loving Creator when so much that is obscene and violent is prevalent in the world? How can we go on believing that things can be transformed, remade, that there is a chance to begin again? Surely the powers of malevolence have outsmarted us and we should curse God and die?

And yet, I have also witnessed an astonishing, strong, bloody-minded determination among those who by rights should have given up long ago, and a true, patient solidarity of ordinary people and faith communities who have made it their mission to travel alongside those who have experienced trauma and abuse. So, if I had to summarize what it is that helps people '*sur vivre*', I would say that there are a number of factors that contribute to their chances, but mostly it is about a deep, powerful will to live that seems to be implanted at the heart of what it means to be a human being.

Alongside this core strength, there are other factors that increase the chances of people transcending the experience of violations. Primarily, I think, the presence of supportive, attentive communities of solidarity is key to this process. Because abusers systematically isolate and groom their victims, there is an inevitable sense of being totally alone and abandoned. The necessity for strong, embodied communities of solidarity to support those who are unable to ascertain what is 'normal' becomes a crucial factor in the process of '*sur vivre*'. These communities may be self-help groups or campaigning organizations, but they might just as easily be a network of friends or supportive family. It is critical that, in a society where the individual is seen as paramount, the Church and other individuals and communities embody a different way of relating in which people will discover a safe enough space in which to let their stories surface. These communities of loving attention need to be very ordinary and very wise. It is no longer acceptable to have our heads buried in the sand and pretend that abuse does not happen, even in our own families. In every church congregation – indeed, in every gathering of humans – there will be survivors of sexual abuse, of domestic violence and other violence. This is not a call to panic, but to be real. We must state unequivocally that such violations of humanity are an atrocity before God and we must put blame firmly where it is due, namely with the perpetrator. We must shift the balance of power in our liturgies to give firm signals that we are only guilty for the sins we have actually committed and we must open up places of attentiveness in which those unheard stories can emerge and receive honour.

A crucial factor in maintaining church communities of solidarity is the education of leaders, particularly clergy, in an awareness of appropriate boundary setting and in what constitutes good practice. We must train our leaders in proper patterns of accountability, for their own safety as well as everyone else's, and make sure that those who are most vulnerable are protected from harm. There is not yet a 'code of good practice' for ministers in the Church and there has often been a fudging of pastoral boundaries which has been destructive or even abusive. Clergy are given intimate access to people at times of profound vulnerability which is both a privilege and a responsibility. Pastoral training for clergy needs to alert them to their personal responsibility to maintain appropriate pastoral boundaries. Clergy abuse is never excusable in any circumstance, and clergy who abuse have no place in the Church. If churches are to be safe enough spaces for people to '*sur vivre*' it is not going to happen by wishful thinking but by intentional steps to bring about space for attentiveness in an atmosphere of respect and trust.

Churches, and clergy in particular, need to know what they cannot and should not be doing. Most clergy are not counsellors or trained psychotherapists. There are times when people with specific professional skills need to be brought alongside pastoral situations to bring insight and experience and sometimes clinical expertise. People are not helped to '*sur vivre*' if they simply fall into a pit of other people's incompetence.

The education and awareness of church leaders and members is key to maintaining churches as communities of solidarity, but these communities take many shapes and forms. This is why the work of places such as Holy Rood House is so important, offering Christian hospitality and welcome. Thank God for the support of the Epworth Fund, for the hard work and vision of Revds Elizabeth and Stanley Baxter and for all those who dedicate their time and energy to make Holy Rood House a safe enough space for stories to be honoured and heard. Alongside time for talking with trained counsellors, therapists and clinical staff, guests are able to find space for their stories to surface and to be nurtured in their path to healing and wholeness. This holistic example of solidarity with those who are emerging from underneath traumatic experiences is an embodied expression of the love of Jesus, in ordinary yet transformative ways, and yet such organizations must fight for funding as if they are 'added extras' to the mainstream life of the Church. On the contrary, they are central to the mission of the Church, offering unique places of solidarity and attentiveness to those who may feel on the edge; surely this is the very heart of the message of Jesus?

Communities of solidarity may take a more formal stance, paying professionals to listen to stories to collect evidence and witness statements. In Chile and Argentina I visited human rights organizations that try to piece together individual stories so that the horrifying experiences of individuals who were imprisoned, blind-folded, raped and tortured can be put into some kind of context. This is painstaking work, but bit by bit stories are compiled and then compared so that the overall truth can come to light. This may lead to court cases in which perpetrators are brought to justice, but will anyway lead to the sense of victims being heard, believed and understood – which, as we have discovered, is so key in the process of '*sur vivre*'.

In South Africa the communities of Khulumani and Volmoed are radically different in their approaches – one is black-led and focuses on the townships of Johannesburg, the other is set among the hills in the wine-growing region south of Cape Town – yet each longs to bring stories of oppression to light, to be alongside others in their truth-telling process, to be attentive to the context in which they work. Each in their own way seeks to offer a new perspective to those who have been in danger of being overwhelmed by their ex-periences, and each encourages encounters between people who are radically different so that new communities of honesty, trust and reconciliation might emerge.

Communities of solidarity are not necessarily groups of people with similar experience or even professionals; they may simply be warm, attentive friends who are unconditional in their regard and yet wise enough to know when additional support is required. They are also people who enable those who have experienced trauma to have a sense of being held within a bigger story. This has been particularly apparent in those places which I have visited that are breaking free from political oppressions. The struggle in South Africa meant that while conditions were abusive, terrifying or destructive, there was also a sense of resistance that was held within a bigger community story rather than by individuals alone. As for the slaves of North America, the biblical motif of exile was strengthening to the sense of being part of an enslaved but coherent people.

This understanding of being part of a bigger story may come from communities of solidarity, but sometimes and mysteriously it seems to be simply a gift from God. The woman I mentioned previously who had never been held by her mother talks of a sense at a very early age that 'Jesus was my friend' despite the fact that she had never been taken to church. I gather that this experience is not unusual. The presence of God at the heart of terror is not everyone's experience; some may feel totally abandoned by God, but I am reminded of Alison's belief that God was beside her on the bridge. We can ask why God didn't stop her jumping, but also wonder at this extraordinary sense of the divine when everything else has disappeared.

Maybe most crucially, people are helped to '*sur vivre*' if someone, somewhere, lets them know that they are lovable, valuable and believable. Thank God, most people grow up being the apple of someone's eye, but for those who have suffered childhood abuses, who live in fragmented or unattached worlds, those messages are hard to internalize. As the counsellors at Holy Rood House know only too well, those who from an early age have never known who is safe to trust or have developed strategies of withdrawing from reality when it has become too traumatic, often arrive at the door without any self-worth, full of unwarranted guilt or unable to form good relationships. '*Sur vivre*' is not an event, it is a long, laborious process in which, piece by piece, a person begins to discover what has happened to them, who they are now, and who they are becoming. It is a transformative process – tender, fragile, precarious and, yes, occasionally quite wonderful.

So, at this point, where words are about to run out, I finish with some images, but first, to take leave of our journey with Luke, on the day of Pentecost (Acts 2.1–41).

\*     \*     \*

It was morning time in Jerusalem and the disciples were staying together in one house, waiting and wondering as they had been instructed. They were not a noble band of upright citizens but a rough-cut, struggling, hurting bunch of humanity whose hopes had been dashed by seeing their leader killed by the occupying forces and were now hiding in fear of their lives. They had denied their allegiance when under pressure, had lied in witness statements and resorted to violence to save their own skins. And yet they were together, a community of solidarity, staying in the same house, and hanging on to each other and to God – this great, silent, absent God, who had left them high and dry and yet of whom they had caught sight in the person of Jesus. That is why they were holding fast, to face persecution, imprisonment, death – yes, but also because there had been rumours of resurrection, of new life. Only rumours, mind you, no hard-and-fast evidence, just fleeting glimpses that all might not be lost.

Then, as if their hearts had been touched with flames, they all burst out talking at the same time, a kind of ecstatic babble that bore no resemblance to everyday language. Words that bubbled up out of their hearts, a sense that something new was happening – something wonderful, a new language that was about to transform everything they would do and say.

Then, later, in the city square, this ramshackle band of disciples experienced something else. The crowd of people that had gathered in Jerusalem from all over the place began to understand them as if they were speaking in their native tongue. It was as if God had broken God's silence, not by a mighty acclamation from on high, but by the transformation of ordinary human beings in the to-and-fro of speaking and being understood. The Spirit was opening up the crack between words and attention, giving a new possibility of understanding in which this silent and disheartened bunch was finally being heard. They may have been speaking seemingly incomprehensible utterances that were welling up from the depths of their being, but the ears of the listeners were able to discern what was being said, each in their own language, and because of that all (well, many) were transformed.

*          *          *

It is Thursday in the Plaza de Mayo in the centre of Buenos Aires, and the mothers and grandmothers of the 'disappeared' are putting on their white headscarves and preparing for their weekly march. They have all lost somebody, and most have also experienced their own traumas. Some grandmothers are still searching for their lost grandchildren who were born in prison after their daughters had been raped or shot. Their grandchildren have been sent to families for adoption, God knows where. The women are coming to the square to be with the lost ones. They have come to this place for 30 years, sometimes rounded up by the police, sometimes facing charging troops, on occasion fleeing for their lives towards the cathedral which on occasions has locked its door against them. But the mothers and grandmothers do not come to the square simply to be sad. They come so that things will be different. Some take on the dreams of their lost sons and daughters and campaign for social reform, challenging the government on controversial issues. They have even founded their own university. The mothers and grandmothers are an embodiment of resilience, of what it means to '*sur vivre*' not by forgetting their story of suffering and loss but by speaking out of their pain and becoming radical but peaceful agents of transformation.

*          *          *

It is mid-afternoon in a township outside Johannesburg. Two theological students from Hartley Victoria College in Manchester are sitting with a group of women who are making bread and stew to feed the 400 men, women and children who will come later with their empty sandwich boxes, or if they don't own a sandwich box, will come with an empty carrier bag. Each will receive bread and stew, spooned into their containers from huge vats. It will feed them, their families, maybe for the rest of the week. Many are children living alone; AIDS is killing 1,000 people a day in South Africa at the moment. The food is not enough, but it's what these women can do to help their community '*sur vivre*', and for the two students who sit among these amazing women, life will never be quite the same again. I know, because I've been there too.

*     *     *

It is 9.30am in the middle of Liverpool, halfway through the year designated as European Capital of Culture, and the city-centre clergy and chaplains are having their weekly prayer time in the café of the new John Lewis store. From the pristine interior we look across the Mersey to the Pier Head where, through the centuries, people have arrived in the city to begin a new life, either seeking their fortune or fleeing from famine. We pray for our city, while early shoppers come to investigate the new precinct and sit at neighbouring tables enjoying an early-morning snack. One of the city-centre chaplains will go on to St John's Market, which is struggling with a different kind of redevelopment; another will go to the old Lewis's store, which has been left high and dry as the city centre has shifted; and I will go to make bread with the street homeless and other wanderers who will find their way to the door of 'Somewhere Else', the 'Bread Church'. Each of us is a member of some small, vulnerable community of solidarity, each endeavouring to hear the stories of the city, and praying that the people here will '*sur vivre*'.

*     *     *

It is lunchtime at Holy Rood House as we begin to plan our second 'Survivor Retreat'. Someone who attended the first one has just sent me an e-mail:

What I have pondered on for a number of years, without coming to any full understanding, is the fact that when Jesus rose from the dead he still had the wounds from the crucifixion, the holes in his hands, feet and side. He could conquer death, defeat hell etc. . . . but the wounds were still there. I wonder about this in my experience. I want to forget about the pain and hurt and the scars that are very deep. I have long wanted things to have never happened. But it seems that integral to resurrection is that the scars and wounds remain?!!? Why? How am I supposed to 'look' then? It must have been important, at the time, as it was commented on and written in the Gospels. Jesus pointed to his wounds as a guarantee of authenticity.

Have you any thoughts on this? Is there a theology on this – why is Christ resurrected with holes and all? What does it mean? What does it mean for me and all those who have been very badly hurt?[2]

I can make some kind of theological attempt at a response here, but am totally aware that words just will not do. What is required in the process of '*sur vivre*' is not that I answer (even if I could), but that I listen, that we all listen, each of us in our own way, that we begin to live these hard, hard questions which are not simply 'for poor survivors' but for everyone. Living with these questions and struggling with what they mean is the very stuff of '*sur vivre*', for us all and for the earth. There is no short cut to a neat theological package, but a wrestling with the very essence of the gospel.

\*       \*       \*

Late last evening, Laura and I shared a meal and a bottle of wine while we looked at the interviews she has recorded in her garden shed on the theme of 'becoming'. One of her interviews is with a young artist who has survived a brain aneurism, who talks about his life as 'intriguing' and his art work as a means to help people be intrigued too. And we talk about the allotment and the passage in Luke's Gospel when Jesus exhorts us to 'Consider the lilies of the field' (Luke 12.22–32). We reflect that this is not simply an entreaty to stare at flowers and give up worrying, but rather to change our lives in such a way that our priorities are set for the kingdom. And I learn that the word 'consider' is derived from fourteenth-century Latin, meaning 'to examine closely'. The Latin '*sidus*' meaning 'star' literally means 'to observe the stars together'. Jesus says, 'Look at the stars together' and find within this a transformation of life that will set new priorities both for you and for the world. This is the radical edge of the gospel, the call to live and to live fully and so to '*sur vivre*', as individuals, as communities, as the earth.

Last week someone who works with refugees told me this story: 'A woman at the project from Namibia was telling me about her detainment in a refugee camp. She had been raped on numerous occasions, and watched her daughters experience the same, beatings and rape. And I asked her, "How did you survive all that, why are you still alive?" and she said nothing, she just got to her feet and danced.'

I hear echoes of the Khulumani song 'God of opportunities, use me', and I am reminded of our last days in Buenos Aires when Bishop Nellie, the Methodist Bishop of Argentina, took us to a project for the homeless in the church where she works. One member of our group was a person who had survived both domestic violence and extended periods of homelessness. We stood together among the gathering of people who had come in from the streets to eat their meal and use the washing facilities in the church; we felt embarrassed not to speak the language and appeared like observers of others' predicaments. Then the person in our party began to speak, while the bishop translated. 'I used to be homeless,' they began, 'I used to beg for food outside the bakers and rummage in bins because I was so hungry. I know what it feels like to sit on the pavement while people look down on you. All I am saying is, you don't have to be looked down on, you can look up.'

And when they had finished speaking, an Argentinian man got to his feet and said, 'Can we dance for you?', and while the bishop led the others in the singing, he and a woman in a large black hat embraced each other and danced the tango. And then they embraced us and taught us too.

> The experience of a globalized world lies in its peripheries, in the moments of risk and change, in the celebration of survival of yet another day.[3]

# Notes

### Chapter 1: The Hearing
1 Churches Together in Britain and Ireland (2002) *Time for Action*, CTBI, pp. 35ff.
2 Hopper, J., website: 'Child Abuse: Statistics, Research, and Resources' (www.jimhopper.com/abstats).
3 Weil, S. (1951) *Waiting on God*, Fontana, p. 114.
4 Morton, N. (1985) 'Beloved Image' in *The Journey is Home*, Beacon, pp. 127–8.

### Chapter 2: The Presenting
1 Creer, M. (2002) *The Guardian*, 14 September.
2 Addley, E. (2002) *The Guardian*, 14 September.
3 Sandercock, L. (2003) *Cosmopolis II – Mongrel Cities of the 21st Century*, Continuum, p. 228.
4 Sandercock, *Cosmopolis II*, p. 227.
5 Dowrick S. (1992) *Intimacy and Solitude*, The Women's Press, p. 14.
6 Chu, J. A. and Dill, D. L. (1990) 'Dissociative Symptoms in Relation to Childhood Physical and Sexual Abuse', *Psychiatry*, Vol. 147/7, pp. 887–92.
7 Mearns, D. and Thorne, B. (2000) *Person-Centred Therapy Today*, Sage.

### Chapter 3: Being Lost
1 Rich, A. (1991) 'Through Corralitos: Under Rolls of Cloud', in *An Atlas of the Difficult World: Poems 1988–1991*, W. W. Norton, p. 48.

### Chapter 4: Boundaries
1 Tate Modern, exhibition leaflet, November 2007.
2 Volf, M. (1996) *Exclusion and Embrace*, Abingdon Press, p. 67.
3 Volf, *Exclusion and Embrace*, p. 67.
4 Ackermann, D. (2003) *After the Locusts*, William Eerdman, p. 15.
5 Ackermann, *After the Locusts*, p. 13.
6 Gorringe, T. (2004) *Furthering Humanity: A Theology of Culture*, Ashgate, p. 1.

7   Magnaghi, A. (2000) *The Urban Village*, Bollati Borighieri, p. 1.
8   See Sandercock, *Cosmopolis II*, pp. 2, 5.
9   Cotter, J. (2000) in *Wrestling and Resting*, ed. Ruth Harvey, CTBI.

**Chapter 5: Breaking the Power**
1   Schüssler Fiorenza, E. (1983) *In Memory of Her*, SCM Press, p. 154.
2   Oxford University Press (2008) *Concise Oxford Dictionary*, 11th edition.
3   Stein, M. (2005) *Foundation Journeys through Care*, York Publishing Services.
4   Colledge, E. and Walsh, J. (trans.) (1977) *Julian of Norwich: Showings*, Paulist Press, p. 315.
5   Grey, M. (2007) *To Rwanda and Back*, Darton Longman & Todd, p. 45.
6   Ganzevoort, R. (2007) *Coping with Tragedy and Malice*, publication pending.
7   Grey, M. (2007) *To Rwanda and Back*, Darton, Longman & Todd, p. 156.

**Chapter 6: Redeeming Relationships**
1   Stein, *Foundation Journeys through Care*, p. 5.
2   Herman, J. (1998) *Trauma and Recovery: The Aftermath of Violence from Domestic Abuse to Political Terror*, Basic Books, p. 160.
3   Sherlock, H. (1983) *Methodist Hymn Book*, No. 774, Methodist Publishing House.
4   Davis, M. (2002) *Walking on the Shore*, Matthew James Publishing.
5   de Gruchy, J. (2002) *Reconciliation, Restoring Justice*, SCM Press, p. 21.
6   Volf, *Exclusion and Embrace*.
7   Grey, M. (2003) *Sacred Longings: Ecofeminist Theology and Globalization*, SCM Press, p. 211.

**Chapter 7: Surviving Church**
1   The Methodist Church (2005) *Time to Talk of God: Recovering Christian Conversation as a Way of Nurturing Discipleship*, Methodist Publishing House.
2   Davis, *Walking on the Shore*.

**Chapter 8: Consider**
1   Miller, A. (2001) *For Your Own Good*, Virago Press, p. 280.
2   *face2face* e-mail correspondence, June 2008.
3   Schreiter, R. (1997) *The New Catholicity*, Orbis, p. 59.